Practical Divining

Richard Foord

Practical Divining

©1997 Richard Foord

ISBN 1 898307 73 3

Cover design by Paul Mason

Published by:

Capall Bann Publishing
Freshfields
Chieveley
Berks
RG20 8TF

Acknowledgments

My thanks go to the many people who have encouraged and helped me with this book, especially David Foord, Tony Foster, David Horsfall, Frank Cusack, John Foord, Peter Smith, Alan Foord, Adrian Schoo, Jill Foster, Ruth Canty, Bill Foord, Katherine Legge, Mal Fields, Len Williams, Ian McNamara of Australia All Over and the staff of the Bendigo Public Library.

Contents

A starting point

"I think, therefore I am."
Rene Descartes, 1596 - 1650

"We hydrogeologists know that electromagnetic phenomena can occur also during the filtration of underground water through rocks. As the water flows around the rocks, the water particles execute complex oscillatory movements. Even here electromagnetic waves can appear, their length depending on the speed of the underground stream. But man's organism, as is well known, is even more sensitive than some physical instruments. For instances, smell allows us to catch the presence of a countable number of airborne molecules of a given substances."

"It is easy to conceive of a man holding a wire rod - a closed oscillating circuit - tuned precisely for the oscillation range of underground water. The human organism simply becomes the signal amplifier as the impulse travels through the nervous system to the hand muscles and the operator, probably unwittingly, turns the rod which thus is most likely something akin to the indicating needle of an instrument."

Professor G.V. Bogomolov,
as quoted in Teknika Molodezhi,
No. 8, 1967.

"It is my conviction that I have received knowledge about archeological artifacts and archeological sites from a psychic informant who relates information to me without any evidence of conscious use of reasoning."

Professor J. Norman Emerson,
Snr Professor of anthropology,
University of Toronto.

Michel de Notredame, 1503-66, known as *"Nostradamus"*

Introduction

Divining has been used by mankind since long before the recording of history began. In the past 200 years it has been investigated by many of the world's leading scientists but still no-one knows how or why it works.

While the majority concede it does work only a few courageous academics have ignored the scorn of their timorous fellows and begun using divining, and also clairvoyance, to further knowledge and understanding in their disciplines.

Traditionally when divining is mentioned people associate it with finding water but among diviners this is only one of many applications of this unique skill.

This book does not set out to promote the ability of the writer, much more importantly its aim is to introduce readers to the some of the areas where divining can be applied to increase knowledge and improve the quality of their lives.

In it I have recorded many experiments and have tried to present the results objectively with equal emphasis on both success and failure.

Consensus holds divining to be an expression of the intuitive mind and as such everyone can develop it providing they are prepared to study, work hard and not be deterred by failure.

Often a diviner feels he or she stands alone. It is at those times it is good to reflect on this advice in Matthew 7:7 -

Ask, and it shall be given you;
seek, and ye shall find;
knock, and it shall be opened unto you.

R.F.

Beware of radiations

Lying snug in bed or dozing in our favourite chair who would think we could be absorbing gamma radiations which could be insidiously breaking down our physical resistance and leaving us prey to such afflictions as arthritis, rheumatism and cancer. Truth or more New Age rubbish? We get enough of the latter these days so it makes one wary about what to believe or reject.

However, I have personal reasons to accept that such telluric radiations not only exist but can cause illness and death. It is incredible that although the deleterious effects of these radiations on all living things have been proven in surveys by leading scientists and medical doctors in several overseas countries no research organisation in Australia is investigating them.

Diviners have led the way in alerting the public about the grave danger from telluric radiations. In 1975 Herbert Douglas, a businessman living Vermont, USA, went to the home of a family whose 12-year-old daughter had double curvature of the spine.

Using a divining rod he found that there were an unusually high number of water veins flowing beneath the house, with 35 of them intersecting under the child's bed. The parents followed Mr Douglas's suggestion of moving the bed and later a doctor found that the curvature had noticeably decreased. Several months later the girl had improved so much she did not need a back-brace as previously prescribed.

In the following year Douglas found intersecting water veins under the beds of 55 patients being treated for arthritis.

In 1978 he reported:

> "*I have now checked 20 cancer cases of different kinds and in nearly all of them got an almost uncountable number of dowsing signals coming from water veins, or less frequently, clefts or breaks in rocky ledges underground.*"

Before World War 11, the British dowser, W.M.Trinder, wrote:

> "*There seems to be very little doubt that rays given off by subterranean water are, if continuous contact is maintained with them, definitely harmful to both human beings and plants.*"

A similar effect was reported by Marguerite Maury in her book, How to Douse.
She states:

> "*Whatever may be the cause of telluric emissions - sheets of water, subterranean streams or dry faults - the effects produced on the health of animals and human beings is nearly always harmful.*"

The French priest, the Abbe Mermet, arguably one of the world's greatest diviners, who pioneered the use of divining in medical diagnosis, stated emphatically that from his experience radiations from water veins were harmful to humans.

> "*(They are) transmitted from floor to floor in any house, factory office as well as in a flat, on the tenth floor of a building. It is in the bedroom that their presence is the most harmful for, in such a case, the individual is not only subjected to the bad effects of radiation, but is also deprived of sound and regenerating sleep.*

6

Impaired health results in consequence, and the affected person suffers from various ailments which neither he nor the doctor can account for."

In the 1920s two German researchers, Winzer and Melzer, found that houses in certain districts of Stuttgart, which had major geological faults under them, had the highest rates of cancer mortality.

In France a physician, Dr J. Picard, had found that over a nine-year period 282 cancer victims had water veins under their houses.

In Switzerland, Dr Joseph Kopp, of Ebikon, a consulting geologist, found that a water vein flowing under a new barn had caused extensive illness to stock.

A survey of 130 barns revealed a high incidence of maladies ranging from severe rheumatism and uterine deterioration to weight loss and miscarriages and calves developing poorly or dying before maturity.

He reported one case of a water vein being found under a pen in which a sow repeatedly ate its litters, while others in nearby pens free from underlying veins, behaved normally. The list of medical doctors and scientists who support the need for research into the harmful effect of subterranean radiations on humans, animals and plants is impressive.

It includes, Dr Wilhelm Von Gonzenback, Professor of Hygiene and Physician in Chief for the City of Zurich, Dr Herbert Konig, author of The Invisible Environment, Dr Paul G. Seeger, former Chief of Cancer Research, Charite Hospital, Berlin, and Ernst Harmann, MD, editor of Weather, Soil, Man.

In 1989, after reading Christopher Bird's reports on deleterious telluric radiations, I conducted a series of tests in the homes of friends and in some I found a large number of water veins under beds and chairs. Mrs Margaret Loughnan, of Dunolly, Central Victoria, reported that since moving into a new house she had developed rheumatism in her right side.

In addition to a water vein being directly under the bed, a water pipe ran under it too. On moving to the other side of the bed the symptoms disappeared.

The next case had tragic implications for myself; John Hammond, who had taught me divining on the family farm at Terang, Western Victoria, in 1936, was found to be suffering from leukemia.

I visited him at his dairy farm at Kotta, Northern Victoria, and found that there were four exceptionally strong intersecting water veins under the side of the bed in which he slept. I pleaded with him to shift the bed and related all the overseas findings but he merely smiled at me. He died a few months later.

I do not claim that these few instances of identifying telluric radiations should be regarded as conclusive evidence of their negative effect on the human body, but they convinced me of the vital importance of the statement by Dr Seeder in 1975.

> "No serious-minded criticism, be it ever so prejudiced, can afford to ignore proofs of the existence of pathogenic telluric influences. Hundreds of cancer institutes all over the world have spent billions without having found any convincing proof of cancers cause. Why has it not been possible to spend a few millions of that huge sum for a thorough investigation of telluric radiation as a prime cause of cancer in human beings. Why has this newly discovered continent of knowledge not been applied to prevention?"

Harmful radiations not only come from underground. There are several sources within the home which should be regarded with care - for instance, television sets and micro-wave ovens. To prove this all a diviner has to do is hold out a wire or pendulum and walk towards either of them. Several diviners I know have got similar reactions to my own - strong reactions two metres in front of a television set and three metres in front of a microwave oven.

The latest craze from the United States apparently is to meditate by placing the bare soles of your feet against a television screen. I was amazed that such stupidity should even be given television reportage time as the practice does nothing more than subject the bloodstream to intense radiations likely to cause cancer. Public and private health authorites warn against sitting too close to television sets.

When I first bought my computer I found that working for extended hours in front of the visual display unit left me with severe headaches and sore eyes. An opthamologist suggested obtaining a low- radiation VDU which I did, and, have not been affected since.

Office staff at Bendigo's Northern District Base Hospital reported that their VDU's gave them sore eyes. The condition disappeared when the VDU's were replaced with later models. Other similar cases have been reported. If these effects are disputed then the question must be asked: why have computer manufacturers replaced old VDU's with low-radiation models? These instances and my surveys are far too superficial to be regarded as hard evidence but they do suggest areas for investigation.

The effect of electro-magnetic radiations from high-voltage power lines has long been a contentious issue. Studies in many countries have proven that people who live or work near such power lines have a higher percentage of certain illnesses than others.

However their findings have been contested by just as many electric power instrumentalities to which the alternative to the powerlines is more costly subterranean cables. A case in point is Studley Park, Kew, one of Melbourne's inner eastern suburbs.

The Victorian State Electricity Commission, which had been a monopoly since its inception in t1919, announced it was putting massive high-voltage lines across the park to help feed the increasing demands of industry in the western part of the state.

However the people of Kew, many of whom were upper-middle class, protested vigorously. This was shrugged off by the commission which proceeded with the power line right up to the edge of the park. Enraged, the people of Kew formed an organisation, *"Powerline Action,"* to fight the issue and battle was enjoined.

The commission was adamant the powerline would go ahead but Powerline Action dug in. The verbal war which raged began to resemble the World War 1 Battle of the Somme.

The SEC formed a battalion of experts, including;

> *"Principal writers, consultants, sub-consultants, designers, typesetters and artists,"*

Commanded by its strategic planning and liaison engineer, while Powerline Action rolled out an even more devastating array of weaponry including health studies in the UK as well as Sweden, which proved the detrimental effects of electro-magnetic radiation.

The government of the day, realising it now had a first-class political row on its hands which could endanger its re-election, appointed a review panel. As with all court cases involving technicalities an expert can be found for and against every argument, but in the Studley Park row the panel was confronted with the highly emotive evidence of overseas research which proved high-voltage electric radiation was detrimental to public health, including facts which linked EMR with cancer in children, chronic depression, suicide and insomnia, some of which were found in tests on animals.

The SEC lost the battle and the powerline went underground. Sweden was the first country to quantify the risks of living beneath power lines, and its National Board for Industrial and Technological Development accepted that such lines could cause leukaemias. It also accepted that a ban on all new housing in areas affected by the radiations was necessary.

Since 1979 scores of epidemiological studies have been published about the effects of electromagnetic radiations, but it was not until two Swedish scientists, Mari Feychting and Anders Ahlbom, produced a dose-response correlation that the danger was finally accepted.

A second study by Birgitta Floderus, of the Swedish National Institute of Occupational Health in Solna, found a link between some forms of adult cancer and exposure to electromagnetic radiations. She connected the radiations with chronic lymphocytic leukemia and brain cancer.

As a diviner I carried out a number of tests under such power lines to see if the electromagnetic radiations affected my responses and found that every time I walked near them I lost all my power to work with either wire or pendulum. In each case I had a strange feeling of inner coldness, no matter how hot the day.

On one occasion I was tracking an object while a passenger in a car and when we came to within about 250 metres of 220,000-volt powerlines my L-wire stopped moving. The driver was an adept diviner and both he and I had the same reaction when we approached the lines.

Later we conducted a series of field tests and found that with an L-wire we could detected the electromagnetic radiations from a 220,000-volt powerline 500 metres away and in the case of 240-volt lines, 30 metres away. Later when these powerlines were drawn on a map and my personal physical reaction was assessed to both by remote divining, deleterious readings were found within 100 metres in the case of the high voltage line and within three metres of the latter.

Experiments with an electric blanket showed the electromagnetic radiations were detectable at 2 metres with strong radiations at 0.5 metres. Radiations from a 60-watt light bulb were detected at 1500mm. These results show only that we as diviners can detect electromagnetic radiations; they give no conclusive indication as to whether or not they have any negative effect on our minds or bodies.

Two cases of electromagnetic radiations interfering with computers occurred at the Footscray Campus of the Victorian University of Technology, to the west of Melbourne. State Electricity Commission engineers found radiations from 240-volt powerlines operating at 50 hertz were interfering with the vertical scan rate of the VDUs which was 70 hertz, causing picture distortion. This was fixed by screening the power lines.

As a journalist I attended several fatal motor accidents and I wondered then whether electromagnetic radiations emanating from petrol engines could affect the brain waves of drivers causing them to fall asleep at the wheel. I was assured by an auto-electrician that as the 50,000-volt sparking of the plugs was totally shielded by the engine casing there would no radiations reaching the driver or passengers.

I tested my reaction as a diviner to a car with its engine running at both idling and cruising speeds and found I could detect very strong radiations at three metres away. This finding was confirmed independently by two other diviners.

When I sat in the front seat of a late model petrol-engine car with its motor running both L-wire and pendulum reacted strongly but when the motor was turned off both became still.

Next day I rang the Ford Motor Company, the Royal Automobile Association of Victoria and the Consumers' Protection Association of Australia but none had investigated the effect of electromagnetic radiations on car drivers. Ford referred me to Associate Professor Harry Watson, deputy head of the Faculty of Mechanical Engineering, Melbourne University, who concurred that radio frequency was a problem in the laboratory and where engines were not enclosed, some instrumentation had to be shielded.

Petrol engine radiations

These radiations are only partly sheilded by the engine block and fire wall

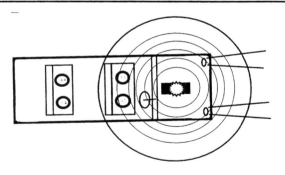

STRONG RADIATIONS - 1 to 2 metres from engine.
WEAK RADIATIONS - Up to 8 to 10 metres.

"Within cars instrumentation has never given us any trouble because the metal surrounds of the engine compartment act as a shield, therefore I suspect one should not be concerned about engine influence.

An area that might be worthy of investigation is the tram, judging by the significant interference the late model version produces on my car radio."

The human brain is a far more delicate instrument than engineering instrumentation and it seems to me that electromagnetic radiations in modern cars, some of which have electrical systems with up to 100,000 volts surging at nearly 5,000 times a minute in a saw-tooth pattern, could have some effect on the the brains of car drivers and passengers.

One auto-electrician told me that while the engine block shielded the ignition systems in these cars, the power lines connecting them to their coils emitted electromagnetic radiations even though they were heavily shielded. This had been proven by holding a portable radio over a car engine which was running.

My interest in locating the source of electrical radiations by divining stemmed originally from investigations I made into a humming noise in an East Melbourne flat. The occupier told me the noise, which had been going on for months, had become like the ancient Chinese water-dripping torture. She said;

"I think I'm going mad,"

When I called at the flat the humming noise was audible in every room. The woman said both the electrical and telephone wiring had been tested but neither caused the noise. When I couldn't locate a source within the flat by divining, I was confident the cause was external.

Some time previously I had participated in a series of experiments in which divining had proven effective in locating the sources of electrical energy in a building. These sources ranged from electrical meter boxes and common domestic appliances to digital watches and even static energy remaining on a hair comb. The sources were located first by the diviner moving around in the room being searched and then confirmed by remote divining conducted just outside the building and then several kilometres away.

My next move was to check the exterior of the client's flat but again I found nothing. Then I went to my car and placing a sheet of paper on the bonnet, I drew a rough outline of the house in the centre of the paper, which I aligned to north, and then by remote divining tried to find the direction from which the humming sound was coming.

At once the pendulum began moving in north-west direction which I marked on the paper. I then drove about two kilometres away where the process was repeated, but this time the direction was north-north-east, which gave an intersection point.

After transferring this point to a scaled locality map I found it was beside a railway crossing. At the level crossing an L-wire pointed directly towards a huge electric supply transformer which was emitting a loud humming noise which seemed to be about the same frequency as that heard in the flat.

I inquired at several houses between the transformer and the flat but the noise could not be heard in any of them. Back at the flat I held out the pendulum and asked only one question: was the humming noise caused by acoustical resonance and the pendulum gyrated strongly in a clockwise direction.

It appeared that by a strange co-incidence the shape of the rooms in the flat were acting like the body of a violin and amplifying the noise emanating from the transformer to within an audible range. As the owners had just bought the flat they did not take too kindly to this diagnosis and I was politely shown the door. Later I sent a detailed map of the area showing the location of the transformer and the flat for them to submit to the State Electricity Commission but I heard nothing further.

This lack of feedback on divining surveys, which has been experienced by most diviners in their careers, is most frustrating for being told that a mistake has been made is often more valuable than receiving a pat on the back.

Water, water everywhere....

My first display of natural ability was in music. Some relative who must have hated my parents gave me a metal drum for Christmas and a sheet of paper with fly spots for quavers and semi-quavers over it.

For days on end I sat in the fork of a tree near the back door of our home in Terang in Western Victoria playing Beethoven's Piano Sonata No. 23, followed as an encore by Tchaikovsky's 1812 Overture Opus 49 - with one stroke of the drumstick for every black dot.

One day I couldn't find the drum and my music had disappeared. I alone was heart-broken.

Our house was next to the Terang school as a result of which our family made friends with people who owned a mixed farm some five miles away. This friendship which was to last for two generations, was strong enough to endure the Foord family's frustrated musical genius, who had turned to singing to further his musical career.

I can remember sitting in a cosy niche on top of a haystack near the house rendering operatic arias by the score, or lack of score. After some weeks of hearing "*For God's sake shut up*," instead of ecstatic "*Encore, Encore,*"

I decided to follow the farmer's 20-year-old son, John, around to see what he did. And follow I did with one small gumboot in every footprint he left until one day in desperation he seized a piece of fencing wire and showed me how to find water. While thus occupied I heard his pony dashing off down the road. And so began my career as a diviner. My singing career, incidentally, reached its zenith later in New Zealand when I started rendering "*Boots Boots Boots,*" a Peter Dawson classic, while working next to a trainee operatic tenor. He interrupted me by saying:

> "*Richard, you have a unique voice. You're the only person I've ever heard who can sing out of tune in five different keys at the one time.*"

A friendship did not develop. The family moved to Melbourne before World War 2 where my growing ability as a diviner was regarded as more of a party trick than a useful skill.

Doing weekend war work on a farm gave me a few opportunities to divine streams but then I virtually forgot about it, becoming totally absorbed in the RAAF, travel, marriage, family and earning a living. I was building a mudbrick cottage at Newbridge, west of Bendigo, when quite by chance I found I could find lost articles with a bent wire.

Working on the Bendigo Advertiser I met local historian, Frank Cusack, and somehow the subject of the occult and divining cropped up. Next day he brought in a book by the famous diviner, Abbe Mermet. I obtained a copy of this wonderful book, one of the best ever written, and prowled the country around Newbridge.

I must have tramped several hundred kilometres through the bush looking for everything, groundwater streams, metal objects left at mining camps, and of course keeping an eye open for the odd nugget or two.

Divining was put to practical use on a fishpond I was making. To get the material for the cottage I had a front-end loader dig a big ditch near the concrete slab on which it was to be erected.

When the building was finished I was left with this problem of what to do with this hole which was big enough to hide a VW in. I posed this problem to a couple of friends at the Newbridge Hotel and the idea of turning it into a fishpond came up.

A few bags of cement, a trailer load of sand and not a few buckets of sweat later and the pond was ready for a brace of redfin, the local piscatorial delicacy. Finally I filled it with water and retired to look up a few choice recipes.

Next morning I went out in my slippers to contemplate my masterpiece but the water had gone. A neighbour, who obviously had a BSc in fish pond construction, informed me the concrete was not thick enough so I put on another couple of centimetres but still the water disappeared.

Remembering my divining skill I half-filled the pond, bent a piece of wire into an L-shape and soon found a small underground trickle of water running towards the nearby site of a brick kiln. Eventually I plugged the leak - an air hole in the cement - filled the pond with water for the umpteenth time, threw in a couple of baby redfin and retired to contemplate this now-permanent property improvement.

Next morning I found the redfin floating upside down looking a trifle unwell. Another neighbour, expert in piscatorial culture, who was present at the burial, told me the cement was far too fresh. Eventually I settled for a water-lily which lived to smile happily at me every spring.

After finding the leak I surveyed the rest of the property and found several groundwater streams running down to the river. At the local general store, which specialised in local gossip, I was told all groundwater in Newbridge was salty.

Word of my amazing occult powers got around and another local inhabitant asked me to find a stream under his property which was farther from the River Loddon than mine.

I did this with an experts flair but the only trouble was that I didn't know how to depth groundwater nor check its purity. Believing I had provided him with the answer to his water shortage problem this good citizen grabbed a shovel and for days dirt flew in all directions.

When the hole got too deep to dig he resorted to dropping a piece of metal pipe down it, the weight of which penetrated the soil leaving a core in the pipe which he then extracted. "*Nifty,*" as he was known, was pretty powerful bloke and the deeper his hole went so his muscles seemed to grow, so did my apprehension as to the result.

Finally came the great day - he struck water at about 13 metres. Dropping a small bottle down the hole he pulled it up and in the sunlight it glistened in its pristine beauty. Raising the bottle to his lips Nifty took a healthy gulp, froze, and as he spat, spraying borewater over his boots. At that point I deemed it appropriate to make diplomatic retreat. I was contemplating a swift exit to Buenos Aires when another neighbour called in and said:

"*I just heard that Nifty wants to see you.*"

He'd heard this at the store, which also had a premium on mental telepathy. I was at the packing stage when he strode up to the door, and with a disarming smile simply said:

"*Thanks for trying to help me but it's salty,*"

And gave me a sample to try. A few tins of cold Fosters washed away the revolting taste of his borewater and so I remained in my mudbrick cottage at Newbridge.

Incidentally, anyone thinking about building in mudbrick should realise that each brick, whose dry weight is about 25 kilos, has to be lifted 14 times before it's plastered in place. As my cottage comprised about 2,500 bricks, it required my lifting a total of 875 tonnes which I did in six months, or at the rate of about 33 tonnes a week. To this day I am known in Newbridge as "*Mudbrick Dick,*" if not as a water diviner.

When humans first began to find water by divining is not recorded even in legends. However, at some stage in raising their knuckles off the ground they found certain members of tribes had an affinity with water which was indicated by the involuntary movement of a stick or twig held in the hand.

Those who developed this strange and bewildering ability were believed to be in direct communication with a god, and so were called diviners. In most communities they were regarded with a mixture of awe and fear and many of them came to a fiery end as they were adjudged to be witches and warlocks with demonic powers.

The first recorded reference associating a rod and water is in the Old Testament.

Numbers 20, verses 7 - ll read:

> *And the Lord spake unto Moses, saying:*
> *Take the rod, and gather thou the assembly together, thou, and Aaron they brother, and speak ye unto the rock before their eyes; and it shall give forth his water, and thou shall bring forth to them water out of the rock: so thou shalt give the congregation and their beasts drink.*
>
> *And Moses took the rod from before the Lord, as he commanded him. And Moses and Aaron gathered the congregation together before the rock, and he said unto them, Hear now, ye rebels; must we fetch your water out of this rock? And Moses lifted up his hand, and with his rod he smote the rock twice; and the water came out abundantly, and the congregation drank, and their beasts also.*

Until printing began in Europe towards the end of the 13th century divining knowledge and skills were passed on orally, but with the advent of letterpress and woodcut illustrations this information became available to those who could read.

The woodcut shows a cross section of a Cornish tin mine with a diviner using a forked stick to locate ore bodies. Among rural communities, divining became an accepted means of finding underground water and few wells were dug without calling a diviner to select the spot.

Even in today's world of electronic wizardry in which hydrology is now a science, the movement of subterranean water, or groundwater, is still not fully understood, and in rural communities many water drillers continue to use diviners to pin-point bore sites.

It was in the Abbe Mermet's book I first read about long-distance map divining. The College of French Marists at Popayan in Colombia, South America, had written to him asking if he would visit their mission as it might have to close through a shortage of drinking water.

Unable to leave his French diocese the Abbe asked the rector of the college to send him a map of the property. After surveying this with a pendulum he advised the rector that if a well were dug in a certain place an adequate amount of potable water would be found. This was done and the well filled with fresh water as predicted. Subsequently the Abbe received the following letter which reads in part:

> *"I have great pleasure to inform you that the water indicated at a depth of 28 metres on a plan of our property at Popayan has been found exactly at the depth indicated."*

(signed) Hermano Anaclet, Rector.

Knowing that Portland in Western Victoria obtained its fresh water from several bores I made a similar survey on a map of the town and found what appeared to be a subterranean river running under it.

Also I found a straight line which appeared to be something metal projecting into Portland Bay. Without much confidence in my findings, I posted the map to Portland's water supply engineer, who returned it to me indicating that the city's three bores were located directly over what had I had shown as a subterranean river. Beside the straight line he had printed: "*A discontinued drainage pipe.*"

Looking back I think this was one of the most exciting moments in my divining career as it proved I could divine remotely using only a map and pendulum just as the Abbe Mermet had done.

When you think of it, all divining is remote. Even when you are standing directly above an underground stream you are remote from it, even if only by a few metres. When next in Portland I mapped the route of the underground river in detail including all the side streams emanating from it.

From the engineer I learned that each of the city's bores were more than 1,400 metres deep (about 4,500 feet) and that the water pumped from the bores reached the surface at 52 degrees C. and had to be cooled before reticulation. He could not tell me why the bores had been sunk so deeply when the top of the groundwater table in the area was within about 30 metres of the surface.

Neither could he explain how the water drillers knew exactly where to spud-in their bores. The engineer suggested I might obtain the information from the headquarters of the Rural Water Commission in Melbourne.

The Rural Water Commission, one of the first Victorian Government departments to be decentralised, was far from the madding crowd in the dormitory suburb of Armadale, and when I parked my car in the tree-shaded road outside I couldn't help thinking what a wonderful escape from the bureaucratic mayhem of Melbourne's central city life. Remote from the roar and frenzy of traffic, the long low buildings slept quietly amid flowers and lawns in the soft sunshine.

As I wandered - one could not hurry in such a somnolent atmosphere - I half expected a calf or lamb to come wandering lazily around the corner.

Inside the building there was cathedral silence. Feeling an intruder, I scanned the notice board and quietly climbed the stairs to where the groundwater department existed. It consisted of a large open office broken up into small chapels by pastel-coloured dividers. Each was equipped with its own altar covered with paper-filled wire baskets and standing impassively beside each were grey multi-draw filing cabinets. Pinned to the dividers were a kaleidoscope of statistical charts like miniatures of the windows in Chartres Cathedral.

In this reverend setting there was only one thing missing - people. I wandered up and down the central aisle as lonely as a cloud, but every desk was empty. It was a setting for the film "On The Beach" and only needed the appearance of Gregory Peck and Ava Gardiner to complete the scene (Ava Gardiner - Frank Sinatra's former wife - endeared herself to Melbournians by saying of this fair city: "A great place for filming the end of the world.")

Then there came a sound. Clink. Clink. I crept down the centre aisle and peering over a partition, saw an incredible sight - homo sapient in deep concentration. Loath to interrupt the stubby finger plodding down the racing page of the morning newspaper, I waited patiently for a while then coughed.

The owner of the finger looked up and keeping it anchored to the fourth race at Flemington gave me an inquiring look. After I recited my query about groundwater depths at Portland, there followed the slow mastication of a coffee cream before a reply was vouchsafed.

"You'd better come back later. They're at morning tea."

The moving finger then moved on. Later, when the rest of the staff returned they tried hard to be helpful but none knew anything about Portland water bores.

Eventually I was directed to an hydrologist from whom I gleaned that a line of water bores were being sunk in a north-south line in North-Western Victoria to test the extent of the groundwater table there but when I mentioned Portland the officer scratched his head. *"Before my time,"* the hydrologist said,

"Why don't you try Portland's water supply department?"

And so this line of inquiry fizzled out. However, refusing to be beaten, I decided to make an on-the-spot divining survey around Portland to see if I could find the origin of its groundwater river.

This revealed that it seemed to be part of a huge interlocking groundwater system of subterranean rivers, streams and soaks which extended through a subterranean sump near Ouyen in North-west Victoria into Southern New South Wales where it ended at the western watershed of the Great Dividing Range.

I was able to obtain some reject maps of Australia from a map printer in Melbourne and enlarged my survey to cover the whole of Inland Australia.

The result was the discovery of several similar groundwater systems which generally flowed from the north and north-east to discharge into the Southern Ocean in the Great Australia Bight.

When I raised my findings with hydrologists in several states they were declared to be ridiculous. When each learned I found the groundwater systems by divining was I was lectured on this being *"unacceptable in scientific circles."*

On a visit to Port Fairy I happened to be in the public bar of the Commercial Hotel, the local maritime conference centre, when a fisherman remarked that a mate of his had found fresh water about 20 kilometres off the coast. He said;

> *"If he wanted fresh water all he had to do was to toss a bucket over the side,"*

Thinking that my dorsal fin was being pulled, I checked this with several other fisherman who confirmed the story. I went over large-scale maps of Australia's southern coastline with a pendulum and found there were at least seven other places where freshwater discharged offshore. I traced these back towards the land where they linked with the groundwater river systems.

Perhaps it would be helpful if I explained my conception of a groundwater river system. I see it as groundwater which moves in different quantities through geological formations at alternating depths and at speeds which vary according to the permeability of those formations.

In some structures, such as limestone or granite, the groundwater can gush through holes or fissures at high speed, like surface streams or even rivers, while in others, such as in sand beds, the movement may be incredibly slow, even measured in centimetres a year.

Over the next few years I carried out many surveys of the inland and coastal regions and the evidence of national subterranean river systems accumulated.

Along the coast were springs which flowed throughout the year, drought conditions not with standing, underground lakes, and Aboriginal water-hole which never dried up. In the centre of Lake Eyre, a huge salt lake in South Australia, a fresh water spring bubbled up continuously.

In 1990 an employee of the Northern Territory Main Roads Board, Noel Marsh, sent me some maps of the area around Tennant Creek, some 500 kilometres north of Alice Springs, for me to conduct a remote survey of the area. He needed to know where underground streams were as he had to drill them to get water to make roads. I marked the several streams on the maps and also what I believed to be part of the national groundwater river system. Here is an extract from his reply:

"I was surprised and pleased to find I could locate all the streams marked on the map starting from Walhallow Station on the Tablelands Highway and heading north. Because of the scale difference I expected to find some variation on the stream sites but all were close to or within 200 metres of the locations marked on the map.

The depths marked on your map were close to my estimates. The estimated flow rate differed slightly on some of the streams but not greatly. I have since drilled a bore close to the above sites and struck water at 110m and continued on to 140m for a flow rate of 3 litres per second. I pumped this bore for six weeks for use on road works averaging 50-60,000 gallons per 24 hours (225,00-270,000 litres). We pumped in excess of 3,000,00 gallons (13,500,000 litres) over this period.

All in all a very creditable performance in remote divining on your part, Richard. The main aquifer marked on your

*maps with its origins in the Great Dividing Range I found
where the map said it would be and the depth and flow
rate are very close to the map specifications. I have traced
this stream towards the WA border during which it
increased from 5 litres per second to over 12 litres per
seconds. I was very impressed by the accuracy of the map
on this one."*

Signed: Noel Marsh.

As drillers are obliged to notify a government authority about
the nature of core samples and the results of drilling, the
correlated results, while giving a general picture of the location
of groundwater, do not show either its origin or direction of
movement.

It is the existence and flow of small streams which has always
interested diviners as these are sought mostly for domestic,
stock and agricultural supplies. While hydrologists have a
comprehensive knowledge of localised bodies of groundwater
and their recharge zones, generally they reject the idea of a
national or intercontinental movement of groundwater.

My remote divining surveys of the Himalayas and Hindu Kush
mountain region and the Tibetan plateau revealed vast
subterranean movements of groundwater which finds its way to
the China Sea, and under India and Pakistan to the Middle
East and North Africa.

The surface river systems fed by these watersheds are
inadequate to carry the colossal quantities of water from
permafrost melt and snow and rain precipitation. Recently I
asked a university lecturer in hydrology for information on
groundwater in Australia and posed instances which seemed to
indicate the movement of groundwater over vast distances. The
text of my letter read:

"At Portland, Western Victoria, reticulated water supply is pumped from three bores which are nearly 1,000 metres deep. In several places in Central Australia petroleum bores have located water at similar depth. In the goldmining region of South-East Australia many deep mines have had to be abandoned at about 1,250 metres because of the inrush of potable water.

Even the most powerful modern pumps cannot hold it at bay. There are many instances of petroleum bores striking water at similar depths. As these depths are far below local groundwater basin levels, the question arises where does the water come from. If water can migrate long distances then this could explain several typical instances of water rising from deep within the earth without explanation.

Potable water of high purity is pumped from wells under Mecca in Saudi Arabia, and water of similar quality flows from a deep-seated spring under an oasis in Libya. Neither of these places have water tables and there are no mountains within reasonable distance which could collect precipitation.

In Syria the Ain Figeh Spring provides water for the entire city of Damascus at the rate of 8.63 m3 per second, and again its source is unknown.

Excavators digging the foundations for a multi-storeyed building in Fifth Avenue, New York, split a rock releasing a enormous flow of fresh water which required the building to be ballasted to keep it in place.

I realise these few instances cannot be construed as a premise to support an argument for the existence of ultra-deep aquifers but they do raise questions as to the origin of the water, and the possibility that it could have come from far distant sources, possibly even many hundreds of kilometres distant. Could not the Hindu Kush and the Himalayas be the source of aquifers who arise in the Middle East?

The reply was another lecture on hydrology designed to correct my lamentable ignorance about the nature, existence, movement and extraction of groundwater and geology in general. On the intercontinental origin of Saudi Arabian groundwater it explained this away as originating during the Ice Age (10,000 - 1.8 millions years ago) and groundwater under Libya apparently originating in the Pleistocene Age (1,000,000 years ago.) It further stated:

> *"There is no possibility that these aquifers could have been recharged from the Himalayas or Hindu Cush (despite popular myths to the contrary) since there are profound geological discontinuities between the two areas. In any case there are chemical, geological and isotopic arguments that prove a Western Arabian origin for these waters."*

Obviously the writer didn't think much of divining as this was covered with the following broadside:

> *"Dowsing or water-witching has been practiced since ancient times by those claiming to have a 'special gift'. Such practitioners range from well-intentioned but mistaken people to cynical charlatans and worse. The method traditionally uses hazel twigs or wire rods, held in both hands, to indicate where best to drill or dig for water. Dowsing has also claimed success in the location of buried objects, ore bodies, etc.*
>
> *There have been various scientifically controlled experiments to test this practice but in every case there has been no statistically significant rate of success. If the criterion for successful dowsing is merely the location of groundwater, then, as discussed previously, the probability of success may seem high.*

This is a classic example of where probability alone is meaningless, and can only be correctly interpreted in the light of statistically significance tests, i.e. we need to know the probability of achieving the same success rate by chance alone..

Contrary to widespread popular belief,it is stressed that coincidence (in this case prediction by dowsing vs.success in drilling) will occur in any data set, and does not constitute a sound basis for adopting a dubious and unscientific method of groundwater investigation.

As for there being "*profound geological discontinuities*" between the Himalayas and Hindu Kush and the Middle East, my Macquarie World Atlas shows that between these two areas lies the Arabian Basin a feature of which is the Indus Fan, the apparent bed of a vast river system which existed before the basins subsidence. Between the basin and the Arabian Peninsula is the Owen Fracture Zone which owing to its irregular nature could never constitute an impenetrable barrier to groundwater flow.

Another hydrologist, who had spent several years studying the groundwater in the Great Artesian Basin, agreed that the flow direction of groundwater under the Simpson desert was generally south, but then made this declaration:

Studies have shown that all (his underlining) the water in the Great Artesian Basin originated as rainfall. There is no water from the Great Artesian Basin that enters the Southern Ocean.

Also, the story that one sometimes hears that water comes from Papua New Guinea to the Great Artesian Basin is pure nonsense.

And then from the lofty academic heights came this exhortation which almost had me tugging my forelock:

> *Again I encourage you to try and read and understand the*
> *basic principles of hydrogeology that are expounded in*
> *textbooks you should be able to get through a library.*

I realise the writer of the second letter was trying to be helpful but I wonder how he would react to being treated in such a condescending manner. Is it totally beyond the bounds of possibility that some aspects of the basic principles of his discipline could be wrong? I am reminded of Einstein's famous comment:

> *"I think, and think, for months, for years and ninety-nine*
> *times the conclusion is false. The hundredth time I am*
> *right."*

I envy the hydrologist his confidence in the completeness of his knowledge. It would be interesting to have an explanation as to how the groundwater in the Great Artesian Basin flows southwards when the basin is supposed to be a closed system.

Water in my bath only seems to flow when the plug is pulled out. Has the basin a similar leakage?

Also as for groundwater not coming from Papua New Guinea, I can only say that a divining survey shows that groundwater originating in New Guinea's Gulf area does feed the Great Artesian Basin. This view is supported by knowledgeable people in Blackall, Queensland, where the town is supplied with a constant flow of potable water by two bores which have run continuously through all droughts since early this century.

A third bore flows continuously into an open drain. None of these bores has been the slightest bit affected by the 1994 drought which is particularly severe around Blackall.

Yet another hydrologist suggested to me that proof of the Great Artesian Basin being fed solely by rainfall was that this was balanced by evaporation from the basin. Could it not be that groundwater flowing from bores like those at Blackall and leakage southwards from the basin is balanced by input from an external source, such as Papua New Guinea, which has yet to be identified, giving the superficial impression that the basin is a closed system?

The contempt in which both hydrologists hold divining unfortunately typifies the attitude of many scientists both in Australia and overseas who reject anything which cannot be tested by traditional ' *scientific methods.*' Can absolute validity be placed on any research into the unknown when it is based solely on established knowledge and methods, which, as history has so often shown, have to be jettisoned later as being both inadequate and incorrect?

Those defending the established scientific barricades would do well to consider the following statement by Prof. William A.Tiller, Material Sciences Department, Stanford University, made in the preface to that remarkable book, Stalking the Wild Pendulum by Itzhak Bentov:

> "*The present scientific establishment has grown somewhat fossilised by its current `world picture' and is locked into a view of reality that has outlived its usefulness. It has begun to limit man kind's growth and has so increased its sense of specialisation, separateness, materiality and mechanical computer-like functioning that it is in real danger of self-extermination. Its sense of wholeness and purpose has been severely fragmented as our egos have revelled in the individual power created by ownership of physical scientific knowledge. We desperately need to find a path back to wholeness.*"

The question which all hyrdrologists who oppose divining should ask themselves is whether they are in danger of holding fossilised views about their discipline, especially when so many of their professorial peers in many countries accept divining as a legitimate means of identifying geological phenomena. Hydrologists in particular should be particularly careful about making sweeping statements as much of their knowledge is based on guessing what exists between any given geological structures.

Fortunately there is an emerging bodies of *"feral"* scientists who now regard clairvoyance and divining as invaluable tools in the advance of knowledge. This is so in the Soviet Socialist Republic where in 1968 a group of 236 geologists, hydrologists, geophysicists, biophysicists, medical doctors, psychologists and physiologists from 98 research institutes and planning bodies all over the USSR attended a conference in Moscow to consider what it termed *"The Biophysical Method"* - a name inspired by the life work of Professor Leonid Vasiliev who specialised for 30 years in the study of telepathic communication at the Institute for the Study of the Brain and Nervous Activity, St Petersburg (formerly Leningrad).

The need for large supplies of groundwater has always been critical in Australia, an island continent about the size of the United States with most of it so arid that habitation is confined largely to the southern coastal fringes.

In the 1930's author, Ion Idriess, published a book entitled *"Boomerang"* in which he postulated the idea of building dams to capture the water flowing from the 2,500- kilometre-long Great Dividing Range along the eastern seaboard of the continent into the Pacific Ocean and Tasman Sea, and redirect it back through tunnels under the mountains to feed the waterless inland. It was heralded as a brilliant idea but too expensive and soon forgotten.

Since then far too little research has been done on what happens to the huge amounts of water precipitated on the western watershed of the range, and, as I have intimated there appears to be a considerable amount of assumption in the data on which ground water management in Australia is based.

34

Australia's groundwater systems

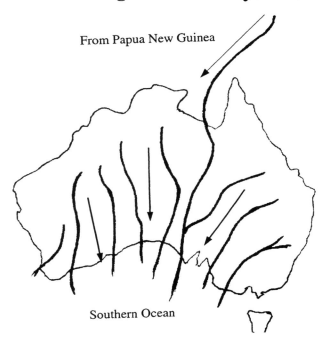

From Papua New Guinea

Southern Ocean

Australia's groundwater resources are fairly well known but there are still aspects where hydrologists have to make educated guesses. Most experts belive that the Great Artesian Basin covering much of Western Queensland and New South Wales is a close system but divining has shown that it not leaks to the south but this loss is replaced with groundwater seeping from the tropical rainforests of the Gulf area of Papua New Guinea. Most Australian hydrologists are contemptuous of divining despite it being accepted by scientists of international standing.

Inland Australia, an area of more than 2.5 million square kilometres, is difficult to imagine if a person has not been through it. Journalist, Dave Horsfall, of Bendigo, has ventured into it many times, even crossing the most arid areas - Great Sandy Desert, the Gibson Desert, the Great Victorian Desert and the Simpson Desert - which cover some 1,000,000 square kilometres.

These deserts and the surrounding land, where temperatures rise to more than 50 degrees centigrade in summer, are harsh and unforgiving and to be careless in them is to die a horrible death. Travellers into these areas must report to the police before and after their journeys but the deserts still claim their victims. Here is how David describes the Dead Heart:

> It is a Divine Sculpture on a magnificent scale. The distances are immense, the vistas breath-takingly beautiful, but the danger is frightening. It is a place of contrasts. In the first place it's not dead but it is the sort of place where men have left their bones to be bleached in the searing sun and polished by the wind-driven sand.
>
> It's a place where everything is larger than life: the heat is greater, the sand is redder, the water less, the dingoes (wild dogs) hungrier and few men go. It's a place were the nights can freeze and the mid-day heat so hot no bare foot can tread on it; where dust-devils coil into the sky and wander erratically across the land, where spumes of dust spurt off the crests of dunes, where the solitude can be almost audible, where water is more precious than food and a man can travel for weeks without seeing another person.
>
> The sight of eagles soaring in the thermals of the day is replaced by the haunting calls of the dingoes at night. It is a place where the stars are lower and brighter and where the ubiquitous colonies of ants outnumber them.

Its has places of incredible beauty - the MacDonnell Ranges, the Olgas, the Uluru (Ayres Rock) complex and Palm Valley, to name a few. However mostly the dead heart is a vast, monotonous plain of red sand and sharp pebbles, and where the Australian eucalyptus trees are replaced by mulga. It's a place where all living things are tested on the anvil of life.

On one occasion we were about 500 kilometres from the nearest habitation when we began to smell petrol. We found that a branch or sharp stone had cut out emergency fuel line and the petrol was leaking into the sand. It was a frightening moment.

On another occasion the engine began to overheat and on opening the bonnet, a cloud of steam gushed upwards. We found a small hole had blown in the water-pump casing. We were lucky we were able to repair the pump for otherwise we would have been on the radio hoping that some one would pick up our distress call. Sometimes such calls are not heard.

Eastern Central Australia is a sump. Into it drains rivers many of which travel underground. The deepest point is Lake Eyre, Australia's largest lake, is 12 metres below sea level. It seldom fills; normally being a vast salt pan which nevertheless contains fresh-water springs which bubble up through the salt.

Despite being a sump much of the Centre is elevated. The low-lying eastern section contains the formidable Simpson Desert and the related Sturt's Stony and Tirari Deserts and rarely rises above 200 metres, but the great deserts of the west (the Tanami, Great Sandy, Gibson and Great Victoria) are between 200 and 500 metres.

The east and west deserts are broken by two blocks of higher country, for the most part between 500 and 1,000 metres. In the southern block the height is 1,439 at Mt Woodroffe, 1069 metres at The Olgas and 867 metres at Ularoo. The northern block, where Alice Springs is situated in a gap in the Macdonnell Ranges, rises to 1523 metres.

As a generalisation the centre can be described as arid (down to an erratic 127mm of rain annually, with an annual evaporation rate of 1270mm). Consistent with the flow of underground rivers and steams there are many wells carrying potable water, some in the centre of the deserts, and a large number of waterholes, many of which are known only to the Aborigines. One such well is Jupiter Well in the centre of the Gibson Desert some 800 kilometres west of Alice Springs and 500 kilometres east of Newman.

A friend of mine had dug the well some years before and had found water at only a few metres deep. Since then a bore had been put down with a pump on top for the use of passing Aborigines.

The water was fresh but warm suggesting that although the bore was shallow the water originates deep within the earth. Near Eucla on the Southern Ocean coast there is a deep cavern in which there is a lake of potable water which stretches as far as lamplight can reach.

Shortly after I had finished this chapter the following report appeared in the Weekly Times in the Jumbuck column written by well known journalist, Geoffrey Wright:

Richard Foord, of Eaglehawk, tells us he is preparing a second edition of his book Teach Yourself Divining. He wants to include the experiences of diviners provided they have been witnessed by an an independent person.

Well Richard, "*Chark*" Chandler, C/o the Royal Hotel, Moulamein, in New South Wales, is just the bloke you are looking for.

And the 'independent person' who has witnessed his divining deeds is none other than Yours Truly. Some months ago, Chark got me to dangle an empty stubby from a bootlace. Then he took me over an underground stream, holding my other hand. The stubby began to rotate so rapidly I nearly became a human helicopter. The shock for this old sceptic was such that I haven't been near an empty stubby since.

Divining has evolved in many directions since mankind first developed it as a practical skill towards achieving a better life but no matter what it is used for in the future its value as a means of finding water for human and animal consumption will always be of great value despite some hydrologists maintaining it doesn't work.

The Australian Sceptics' Society

One hydrologist suggested that I should take up an offer by the Australian Sceptics' Society to pay any diviner $10,000 who could prove that divining works. Acouple of years ago I was approached by a member of the society to undertake such a test and I accepted but on very definite conditions. These included that a test should be :

> * *Conducted on a triple-blind basis, ie - three separate phases supervised by independent panels, one of which would adjudicate the results;*
> * *Undertaken as a genuine scientific experiment;*
> * *Within the scope of divining;*
> * *Conducted in an atmosphere conducive to a scientifically acceptable result being obtained; and*
> * *Not be publicised until after the test was completed.*

As the Sceptics' Society has conducted previous tests as part of a popular television program, which accorded the society widespread publicity, obviously my desire to treat divining as a subject worthy of serious research did not appeal and I heard no more.

Sensitive Hands

Hands have long been key instruments in expressing human sensitivity. The laying on of hands was used by Jesus of Nazareth in healing the lame, the halt and the blind. Touching another person with the hands is the way we all use to express our feelings of love, compassion and friendship. Even a baby does this instinctively when it needs its mother's reassurance.

When we are angry with someone our instinct is to give them a good wallop. In divining we use our hands to hold various tools such as Y-shaped twigs, single pieces of wire, pendulums and L-wires. Once I tried to divine a stream with a long wire strapped to my arm but with limited success.

To contact other diviners and gather information about their experiences for this book I put letters in newspapers throughout Australia and among the many replies was one from a 13-year-old girl from Wodonga in North-East Victoria. She related her father's ability as a diviner then rather casually added that she was able to find underground streams as well. When I read the next four-word sentence my eyes popped. "*I use my hands,*" said Sharon.

If this were true then Sharon had a unique ability which warranted not only inclusion in this book but its own chapter. Sharon said she wanted a copy of my first book "*Teach Yourself Divining,*" so I sent her a copy and asked if in exchange she would write something for me.

In conversations later with her mother, Denise, and her father, John, both confirmed her ability to divine water only using her hands. Here is what Sharon sent me:

Dear Richard:

I'm a 13-year-old girl and I first started to water divine about a year ago.

Our farm in North-East Victoria, where I practice my water divining, ranges from steep to undulating country.

When I practice my divining I am able to use an L-shaped wire, a Y-shaped stick, a bone, phalaris grass and also my hands.

My hands are very accurate. I hold my hands out in front of me parallel with the ground and as I get closer to a stream my hands begin to be pulled down by the power of the stream. When I'm right above the stream my hands will have dropped right down to my legs.

When I first discovered this I didn't really understand it so I asked my father to check my results. All my results were correct and now I am very confident that I can find water only using my hands.

I began experimenting using my hands after I read about it in a book. My sister, Robyn, and I thought we should try it.

I would like to explain how divining began in our family. My father was having some trouble with an irrigation dam so he asked an experienced water diviner to have a look. Dad picked up some hints from the diviner and found he was able to do the same thing. My father now divines for two earth-moving companies.

I have learnt which way a stream is flowing and how to find its depth and strength.

Now I am going to tell you how I find the flow. When I find a stream I stand in the middle of it facing one side and both my hands drop. Then I turn around and face the other side and the same thing happens. The direction from which the stream is flowing is indicated by which of my hands is pulled down the quickest.

There are two methods I can use to find the depth and strength of a stream. When I have someone to assist me I stand in the middle of the stream and hold my hands out in front of me. The other person walks backwards at right-angles holding a open bottle of water.

When the person holding the bottle reaches a certain mark my hands will drop. The distance between this mark and where I'm standing shows how deep the stream is. When the person holding the bottle continues to walk backwards my hands will drop a second time.

The distance from the first mark to the second, which I call the strength mark, shows how strong the stream is. The longer the distance between the marks, the stronger the stream will be. This method can be used with an L-wire and a Y-stick.

If I am alone I use two L-wires.I push one into the centre of the stream and after touching it with the other I simply walk backwards.The wire in my hand will indicate the depth and strength marks.

The only disadvantage in divining for water with my hands is that my arms get tired.

Signed: Sharon McGaffin,

Sharon McGaffin shows how she divines for water

A battle over oil

I have been experimenting with divining for oil for some years and proven to my satisfaction that I can find areas where oil and gas deposits exist. Most die-hard petrogeologists will smile at this brash statement, but before doing so they should read of the work of the American diviner, Paul Clement Browns, who divined oil for some companies they might have heard of, Standard Oil, Signal Oil and Gas, Getty Oil and Rothschild Oil, to name a few.

Knowing that Australia's premier company, the Broken Hill Proprietary was about to begin prospecting in Western Bass Strait I wrote to them asking for help in my research into divining for oil, stressing that I had no designs whatsoever on their "*hip pocket.*" This evinced the following most cordial reply from the company:

As you are aware, the conventional exploration techniques used by the world oil industry have only a very limited ability to recognise hydrocarbons ahead of the drill. It will be interesting to see how (BHP) Petroleum's drilling results fit with your less expensive method of evaluating the BHP permits.

Later BHP Petroleum sent me a map of their two permit areas in Western Bass Strait, Vic/P30 and Vic/P31, and asked me to mark on them areas where I considered hydrocarbon deposits to be. I spent a considerable time in preparing a detailed map-divining survey of the two areas which was duly sent to BHP Petroleum. Then there was silence.

Bewildered that my submission had not even been acknowledged I journeyed some 170 kilometres (with a leg in plaster
through having a bunion orthopaedically removed at the time)
to Melbourne to beard the petrological lion in its den.

A dark grey-suited executive (Why do all businessmen dress
like clones?) gave me five minutes of his valuable time to state
that they had examined my map and it did not coincide with
their scientific evaluation of the prospect areas. With that he
sped through the revolving doors waving to friends with whom
he had a luncheon engagement leaving me holding my coat,
briefcase and crutches to fight my way through the aggressively
revolving door. My Charlie Chaplin exit brought the wry
comment from another executive following me: "*If you had
fallen it would have been a soft landing,*" indicating the
retreating back of the person I had spoken to. On the way home
I could not help comparing my treatment with the courtesy and
encouragement I had received from the first representative of
BHP Exploration.

Sometime later BHP Petroleum announced in the media that
its first well, Eric the Red, had been dry. This failure provided
me with an ideal opportunity to prick the lion in its oleaginous
rump over its reaction to my survey so I pushed off a letter
claiming success for having indicated where BHP Petroleum
should NOT have drilled. This achieved a result which could be
compared to hitting a beehive with a sledge hammer. A letter
from the company burned through the post to this effect:

> "*First, you mentioned that your "survey" of Vic/P31
> matched our own results. I assume this is because (.. I
> omit the name..) mentioned to you that based on a quick
> visual examination there appeared to be some correlation
> between a lead which we had identified and an area
> drawn on one of your maps.*
>
> *Having now spent a little more time examining your maps
> we find there is no valid statistical correlation.*

Secondly there is no connection between the areas identified by you and the prospects which we have chosen to drill. We have made no use of your interpretations in determining where we will drill our exploration wells in VIC/P30 and VIC/P31. We mentioned this because there are some comments in your letter to (..I omit the name..) which appear to indicate that you believe otherwise.

Finally, I believe you may have over estimated the benefit which BHP Petroleum believes it might gain from your continuation of research. We see it as desirable to keep an open mind, but we have viewed the exercise carried out by you in VIC/P30 and VIC/P31 as assisting you rather than likely to provide any benefit to BHP Petroleum in its exploration activities.

Similarly, whilst we suggested that you may wish to test your technique on the producing areas in Bass Strait, in accordance with (..I omit the name..)'s suggestion, please do not think that BHP Petroleum is requesting you to do so or that it wishes to receive the results of such an exercise.

In the light of the information you have provided to us BHP Petroleum does not wish to pursue a `mutual aid research project' with you as proposed in your letter of 7th April, 1992. Nevertheless we wish you well with your investigation."

Isn't it interesting what a world of difference can be given to a word by enclosing it in quotation marks. Would I be wrong in thinking that the writer doesn't think much of divining? Despite the preamble in my original letter to the company that I was not wanting to *"dip into their wallet"* I suspect the company had become concerned that if my predictions were proven correct I might claim a production royalty similar to that which back in 1960, they agreed to pay an American petrogeologist, Dr Lewis Weeks, for the discovery of the rich oil and gas fields in Eastern Bass Strait. A world-wide media headline: "*Old Age Pensioner claims multi-million dollar royalty from BHP*" would give even the most insensitive exploration executive a nightmare.

An interesting ending to this story is the announcement by BHP Petroleum that its Minerva field - which was marked on my survey map - was estimated to contain 500 billion cubic feet of gas, or, in their own words, enough to service Victoria's total gas market for about two years. This conflicts with the company's statement that - "*there is no connection between the areas identified by you and the prospects which we have chosen to drill.*"

The map on Page 49 shows my survey of the Minerva field submitted to BHP and that their holes, Minerva No's. 1 and 2, fall within it.

Any reasonable reckoning would regard this as a good result especially considering that the world oil industry's success rate in drilling producing wells is about three in every 100.

However diviners are also far from infallible as demonstrated with BHP's La Bella field which I missed altogether. After this well was announced I surveyed the area again and was able to see my mistake. It does seem a pity that while in several overseas countries divining is acknowledged as having proven an extremely useful aid in both subterranean and submarine explorations, in Australia it is generally rejected out of hand.

Otway Basin oil/gas searches

SCALE |———— 2500metres ————|

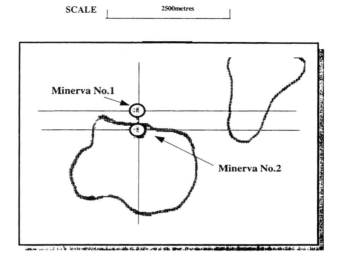

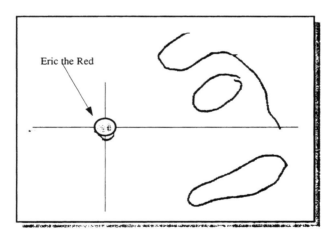

Producing well drilled in the Otway Basin shown in relation to outlines of deposits identified in early experiment in remote map divining. The search missed a third well, La Bella.

I consider divining only an aid to orthodox oil prospecting and do not claim it is an alternative to methods now being used. Further research has shown that although it is unreliable for estimating the precise nature of deposits, it seems to be an extremely, fast and accurate means of targeting areas for detailed analysis and therefore, could save oil companies much time and money.

This is especially important when the success rate of drilling is about 1-in-4 in Bass Strait and about 1-in-70 world-wide.

When I began divining for oil I wrote to several companies asking if they would help me in developing the divining detection technique but none bothered to reply.

However I can well understand how galling it must be to professional petrogeologists, some of whom have a lifetime of study and research plus many years in industry, to be told by a unlearned diviner that he knows more than they do. Perhaps it is pertinent to remind people who have such a prejudice towards divining to recall Einstein's comment about electricity:

"We don't know what it is, but as it's there, let's use it."

In the 1970s a Bavarian engineer, Jacob Stangle, who had personally investigated cancer deaths which occurred above groundwater streams, built a device which measured the gamma ray radiation which is constantly emitted from subterranean geological structures. When this device traversed underground streams it produced strip print-outs showing the intensity of the gamma radiation was much higher over the streams than in adjacent areas.

As the radiations recorded by Stangle were identical with similar radiations identified by diviners it seemed sufficient proof to pursue researching divining to establish the specific areas in which it could be used effectively. A specific statement linking subterranean isotopic radiation with hydrocarbon deposits was made by Dr Armin Bickel, a former NASA scientist, who said:

"Constant changes due to crystallisation in geological formations that have been going on for half a million years can, through isotope detection, provide clues about what lies below. Oil and gas bearing formations act as buffers to block normal radiation issuing from geological structures below."

My own experiments in divining for oil began some years ago when I was holed up in a motel in the Western Victorian seaside city of Warrnambool. I was there on a business trip but being winter and with freezing rain squalls battering the city direct COD from the Antarctic, I settled for the warmth of the motel room complete with *"Colour TV, Videos and Instant Room Service"* - just like home.

Having watched a re-run of a re-run in which some Texan roughnecks had a shoot-out over an oil gusher, I began to wonder if there were any oil deposits near Warrnambool. So I squelched downtown, bought a survey map of the hinterland and laying it on the coffee table I commenced to go over it with a small pendulum proceeding outwards in concentric semi-circles.

The pendulum gave several indications of what appeared to be deposits of hydrocarbons with the strongest coming from some 45 kilometres to the west near the village of Yambuk. Realising that if any oil or gas had been found in the area locals would know, I rang the Yambuk store and an excited owner told me that an oil company had drilled two holes on the farm owned by Calvin Hocking, some 15 kilometres to the north and one had been "a gusher."

Next day I drove to the farm and on the way I steered the car with my right hand while I held a divining wire with my left. About seven kilometres south of the farm I got the typical kick indicating an energy line. During the next two hours I traversed all the land around the farm until I had mapped what I thought were the limits of several small petroleum deposits, some of which seemed to extend under the property. Then I drove up to the farm but no-one was there.

Following the direction given by my L-wire I came to a substantial barbed-wire fence and I could go no farther. Looking around for bulls towards which I had proven little compatibility, I scaled the fence and began to walk northwards.

After negotiating several other similar fences and feeling as though I was trying to break into a razor-wired gaol, I suddenly heard the sound of a truck engine. The vehicle, stopped went through several gates and headed straight towards me, its mounting roar boding me ill for I had to admit I was a trespasser caught red handed, or mud-footed, if you prefer. The truck ground to a halt (I've always loved that term) and out came a very belligerent looking farmer. Before he could yell, or even pull out his shotgun I got in first and said: "*Are you Calvin Hocking.*"

Then began a heart-felt conversation during which he revealed that an oil company, with a prospecting lease, had torn aside one of his fences and drilled two wells on his land. One of these wells realised 300 barrels of beautiful gooey crude, of which he had plenty of samples.

Before leaving, the company erected a "*Christmas-tree,*" - the name known in the oil industry for the metal pipe connector installed on top of producing wells - and surrounded it with a fence. The drilling company informed Calvin that he would be paid a rental of $50 a year for the fenced off area. The company repaired the other fences before leaving.

Calvin, who had been cutting and sawing wood on his property to supplement his income, was overjoyed at the oil strike, and to him and his family it was the equivalent of winning the million-dollar lottery. But when he conferred with a solicitor he was told that under an Act of Parliament anything found below ground or in the air belonged to the Crown. He wept, he cried, he damned near died, but to no avail. Some $50 a year rental from the oil company was all he could claim.

The law in respect of below ground-level ownership seems dreadfully unfair and loaded in favour of the big exploration companies. Calvin was able to give me samples of the crude oil, the drilling company's plans of the area and also print-outs of their seismic surveys which provided me with plenty of practice over the next few months.

Then occurred a strange coincidence which seems to happen so often in life. Susan Probert, who had a small property south of Kyneton, some 80k south of Bendigo, rang me and asked if I could find water adjoining her house. "I want pure mountain water and lots of it," she stressed. "I want a river."

Before calling on her I surveyed the whole area by car and on foot but there was no indication of a river. Widening the area of my investigation, most of it done by holding an L-wire while driving the car, suddenly the wire kicked violently. I got out and checking both north and south concluded, indeed, I had found a river.

Calling at the farm I met this delightful lady and she reiterated her need for a subterranean cataract but I had to confess there was none under her property. Just to prove it I walked the property but the result was the same as before - no river.

Susan was a bit depressed at this news and I asked why she wanted to find a river. She said it was to provide fresh water for her family and a few cattle. Ah! A stock and domestic supply. Immediately I started again and found the place was riddled with small underground streams any of which could provide what she wanted.

Over morning tea I told her that the only river I had found was some half a kilometre to the south and she replied:

"Oh, yes. There is a big underground river running through there and it keeps several big dams full."

Reflecting on this later it seemed to me another example of how a diviner can program his or her mind to find a specific target. She and her husband Geoffrey took me to lunch at a nearby country inn, called the *"Pig and Whistle."* Situated about three kilometres away at a crossroads to nowhere it stood surrounded only by farmland, but in its parking area was a stack of cars which would have done credit to a small supermarket.

What a magnificent lunch I was given! We were greeted at the door by the proprietor, who had the same skill as Vincent Rosales of Maxim's in Toorak, of remembering every name he heard. He ushered us to a small table from which we watched the chef carve huge chunks from a hapless porker sizzling on a spit.

During the excellent lunch Geoffrey happened to remark that he was the secretary to an oil search company, Continental Resources, which had an exploration lease in North-West Victoria, PEP 121. This led to my making a remote divining search of the lease which seemed to confirm what had been found in geological surveys.

Geoffrey gave my report to the company's petrogeologist, who sent me a piece of paper on which she had drawn four circles and asked me to state if any of them indicated a hydrocarbon deposit. The only clue to their locations was their approximate longitudes and latitudes. I submitted a report on the test to Geoffrey and then heard nothing more.

Some months later I rang him and he said: *"You've really upset the geologist over that test."* Apparently she had said: *"If he can do that why hire me."* From that point onwards, using remote divining techniques, I ascertained where nearly every petroleum deposit lay in Victoria and visited many of the sites to check dimensions and depth estimates.

On site I followed the same method I had used at Yambuk - criss-crossing the prospect area until I picked up petroleum energy lines, then measuring their distance from the nearest surveyed cross-road and aligning them with the nearest road to check my accuracy. To facilitate these surveys I wore a pedometer attached to my belt which recorded my paces.

I had determined the average length of my pace by walking the fairways of the Marong Golf Course, near Bendigo, and dividing the length of the fairways with the number of steps recorded on the pedometer. One of the few indications of a big deposit was west of the Kerang - Swan Hill area in North-West Victoria where there appears to be a substantial quantity of oil or gas.

Using the same remote divining technique I then covered the whole of Australia, and once again, to ensure that I was maintaining contact with reality, I checked my findings against petroleum survey maps. One interesting fact emerged when I was checking the oil and gas fields in Eastern Bass Strait. With a small pendulum I traced on a virgin map the positions and shapes of each deposit in the field but on comparing my marks with a petroleum survey map I found that my outlines of the deposits were smaller.

Later when discussing this field with a petrogeologist he expressed no surprise at my findings, saying that the survey map had been made when the field had been discovered and now all the deposits were about half the size. In fact the field was expected to become uneconomic within a decade or two. To ascertain if it were possible to remote divine oil and gas deposits in other countries I began checking systematically those close to Australia, gradually extending the surveys to distant countries.

Having long been interested in China having studied the philosophies on which its culture is based, I checked the country from north to south and found indications of big hydrocarbon deposits in the Gulf of China and near Jinan, Heifei, Nanking, south of Xuancheng and in the South China Sea and the Gulf of Tonkin (see map opposite).

In and around Japan there wasn't much to speak of but up in the Sea of Okhotsk there seems to be one deposit worth investigating but it is in deep water. Another continent surveyed was Africa where I found substantial areas worthy of detailed investigation in Libya, Mali, Nigeria, Sudan, Zaire and Nambia and also offshore from Tunisia.

An open invitation

With the mounting evidence that divining skills are effective in locating deposits of hydrocarbons the time has come for prospecting companies and diviners to begin working together instead of wasting their energies in argument. My experience pales beside that of the American, Paul Clement Brown, whose amazingly consistent achievements in locating oil and gas deposits earned him the respect of some of the world's leading oil companies. I hope that in relating my experiences other diviners will be encouraged to develop their skills in this area. Experience has shown divining can only indicate the approximate position of deposits, not their precise nature or extent, but by so doing, it can help localise seismic surveys in a prospect instead of the entire prospect having to be covered. The savings in time, labour and money alone from this assistance would be immense.

I offer an open invitation to any government instrumentality or oil company of any country to join with me in a genuine research project aimed at producing a combined divining-seismic prospecting technique.

Oil/gas deposits in Africa
(Not to scale)

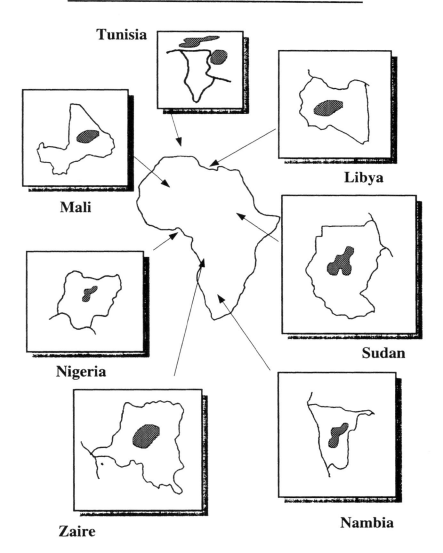

Tunisia

Libya

Mali

Nigeria

Sudan

Zaire

Nambia

China's offshore oil/gas deposits

(Not to scale)

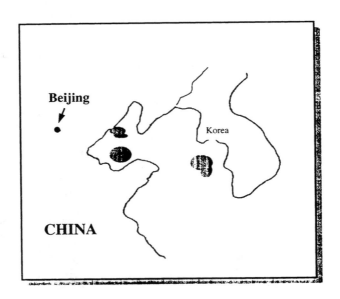

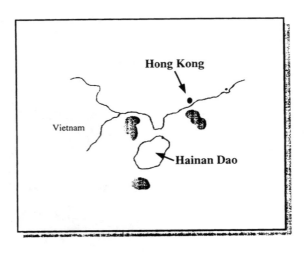

Tasmania's oil deposits

When I was surveying the Bass Strait for oil deposits I noticed that all the exploration companies were concentrating their efforts on Victorian waters. This prompted me to extend the survey into Tasmanian waters and I was surprised to find there appeared to be extensive local fields, one of which was even accessible from the northern coast of the island.

On the next page is a map of my survey showing at least three areas which appear worthy of further investigation by seismic surveying. I sent my findings to the Tasmanian premier of the day and received the bland reply they *"would be borne in mind.."* This political pat-on-the-head turned my thoughts to the economics of Tasmania developing its own oil fields and I soon realised my efforts were pretty pointless and naive.

For Tasmania to develop its own source of oil and/or gas fields it would need the services of one of the big oil exploration and development companies whose interest would be dictated by the existing world and Australian production and distribution of petroleum products. The idea of Tasmania becoming self-sufficient in oil or gas production and possibly competing for local markets would have an interesting effect on its own and the Australian economy.

There is a very strong likelihood of my survey being correct as the area north of Tasmania is sedimentary, similar to the basins extending across the Victorian part of Bass Strait. Also shale oil is found in Northern Tasmania, similar to that found in East Gippsland.

Tasmanian oil/gas deposits

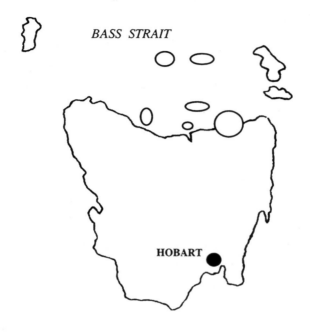

Research has shown that hydrocarbon deposits act as a blanket to normal isotopic radiations. The areas indicated diagrammatically above are where remote divining has shown such reduced radiations occur, and therefore, as they are in a typical oil-bearing geological stratus, they could be worthy of more detailed seismic analysis. The socio-economic implications of Tasmania having its own petroleum oil/gas fields are interesting. Petrogeologists say the southern side of the Bass Strait sedimentary basins is not as rich as the Gippsland area but little work has been done so far to prove them one way or the other.

Nuclear subs skirt Tasmania

As the sea is in my blood, as it were, it was inevitable that many of my divining experiments would be concerned with ships, their whereabouts and their passages. One of my grandfather's was a sea captain, my father was a mate in the P & O Line and I was a seaman for about five years.

One of my sons is also a seaman. This son, incidentally, regards the divining activities of his father with a very jaundiced eye. I sent him the MSS of my previous book on divining and over one chapter he scrawled "*bulldust*." This dealt with my claim that both United States and USSR (now USR) nuclear submarines regularly sailed within 22 kilometres of the southern coast of Tasmania.

May I put my case which I believe is proven, if not by divining, then by irrefutable logic.

A few years ago when the Indian Ocean was the focus of world nuclear strategy and nuclear submarines of all nations played tag between Africa, India and Australia, I became interested in the sea traffic through the Southern Ocean south of Australia. I obtained a large world map and, using a pendulum, began marking on it the tracks of the various vessels which used this passageway. I was doing this largely for divining practice.

Soon it became apparent that there was what appeared to be the regular transit of vessels sailing around the southern coast of Tasmania rather than through Bass Strait. This seemed very odd as it added considerable time and cost to voyages, a factor which commercial shipping lines would not tolerate. I also noticed that none of the vessels called at any Australian ports, a fact I later checked with maritime authorities.

With my interest now alerted, I decided to follow one of these vessels to see where it came from. But this wasn't easy for its track seemed to wander around the Indian Ocean without purpose. However I followed the track of another vessel which I picked up off Cape D'Encastreaux, the southern tip of Western Australia, and marked its day by day passage around Southern Tasmania and then directly north into the Northern Hemisphere. "*Ah,*" I thought. "*It must be making for Japan.*"

This was the route taken by various Japan-bound ships I'd sailed on. However, to my bewilderment it sailed past Japan until it reached the Sea of Okhotsk where it swung left and passed through the La Perouse Strait between the USSR and Hokkaido, and then sailed south-west until it reached the Soviet naval port of Vladivostok.

I realised that unwittingly I had stumbled on a surprising fact for only a Soviet naval vessel would have taken this route. The only alternative was through the Korea Strait which was the territorial water controlled jointly by Korea and Japan.

I then turned back to the Indian Ocean and posed the question: how did the nuclear submarines of Russia and the United States get into this little pond in the first place. The Suez canal was out, as was the Strait of Malacca between Indonesia and Malaysia and Torres Strait between New Guinea and Australia. Also for Russian submarines passage through the English Channel was out, furthermore the route into the Baltic Sea through the Skagerrak between Denmark and Sweden was also in national waters.

Everyone will recall the political furore which occurred when a Russian nuclear submarine suffered a melt-down in one of its reactors in the Skagerrak a few years ago. The Bosporus, crossed by a big suspension bridge was controlled by Turkey, which would not have appreciated nuclear subs negotiating this narrow passageway.

So the second premise in the argument - that both US and Russian nuclear submarines were forced to use the Southern Tasmanian route - seemed to be realistic. Next came checking on the daily passage speeds of the nuclear submarines which used this passageway.

Again using a pendulum I found that the average daily run was about 1,000 kilometres, or about 500 nautical miles, which gave the submarines a speed of about 22 nautical miles per hour (40 kilometres). This was a typical cruising speed of a nuclear submarine on passage.

Today, with the Russians now an ally, there is little need for nuclear submarines to patrol the Indian Ocean with fingers poised above missile firing buttons. However, although the nuclear submarine traffic in the Southern Ocean has obviously become infrequent, there still remains the fact that one of the only two open-sea routes into the Indian Ocean is around Tasmania.

Surely this warrants the Tasmanian State Government demanding that the Federal Government declares that the territorial waters south of Tasmania must extend out to the fishing zone limit of 200 nautical miles south of the Maatsuvker Group and South East Cape. I'm sure no Tasmanian wants to shout a "Coo-ee" greeting to any nuclear sub as homewards it plods its weary way, wherever home is.

Routes of alien atomic submarines

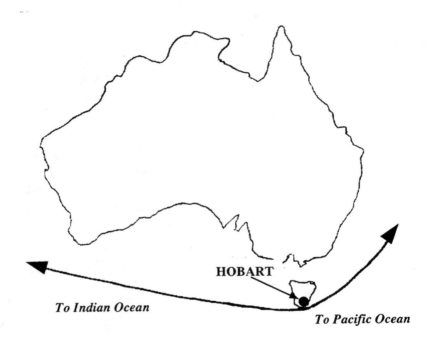

A most remarkable woman

It was hot.

Outside the railway carriage window the flat plains of the Punjab disappeared in the distant dust haze where land and sky became one. In the corner of a private compartment the middle-aged woman leaned back with her head to one side seemingly asleep.

Her husband, a British railway official, glanced up and said: *"Violet, are you awake?"* There was no reply so he continued scribbling the report his secretary would type when they returned to Delhi.

But his wife was far from sleep. With her eyelids divorcing her from the reality of the stuffy carriage, her husband, and the flickering sun-bleached scene outside the window, her mind revolved over an incredible meeting she had had with a Indian fakir under a banyan tree some 30 minutes before.

She and her husband had stopped at Bhatinda, a railway junction in the Punjab, in North-West India, where he had attended an important meeting with local railway officials. She had accompanied him on the journey as it was her duty as the wife of one of the British raj to pay her respects of the local Rani.

After visiting the Rani and enjoying a cold lime drink in the cool, lofty reception room of the palace, she had returned to the train but the carriage was now hotter than when they had arrived. With her broad, loosely woven hat shading her face, and protected by a gay-coloured parasol, she decided to walk along the roadway adjoining the station. By walking at least the air would be moving past her face.

She turned a corner and saw a huge banyan tree some distance away. "I'*ll walk to that then turn back*" she thought. When she got near the tree a patch of white at its base became the dhoti of an Indian fakir who was leaning against one of the aerial roots under the green canopy.

An impulse drew her steps closer to the tree where she stopped about six feet away. The fakir opened his eyes and looking straight at her, said: "*You have come, Memsahib.*"

The woman's code of behaviour, moulded by her British upper-class education, and the standards of deportment demanded of representatives of the British crown, was affronted by the boldness of his demeanour. She was about to turn away but somehow she found that her legs would not move. She looked again at the fakir and his dark eyes held her.

The fakir was thin to the point of emaciation, his face gaunt and lined, his arms narrow stalks at the ends of which lying across his knees were bird-like claws. Fakir and memsahib remained motionless, caught in a world of the mind where time and place had no meaning.

Then he spoke. "*Memsahib, you are worried?*" The voice was deep and vibrant like the sound of a cello, in startling contrast to the spindly frame from which it came. It was the same tone she had heard many times from Indian mendicants as they droned: "*Om Mane pedma Hom Om Mane Pedma Hom.*"

Her answer came spontaneously. "*Yes I am terribly worried.*" Then there was silence, a long silence while the two people one brown and the other white were locked together. The fakir said: "*Give me your locket*".

Pulling off her hat the woman reached behind her neck and unclasped the gold locket which without demur she handed it to the fakir. Still with the woman entrapped in his gaze he held the locket out in front of him where it swayed slightly, twisting and glinting in a shaft of sunlight. Suddenly the locket began to move, slowing at first then with increasing rapidity until it was describing broad circles.

Tearing her eyes away from the fakir's the woman began watching the gyrating locket. After a moment it seemed to grow in size blocking out everything, a whirling golden vortex towards which she was irresistibly drawn, deeper and deeper.

The pulsing, swirling locket was now a golden world and she was part of it. She was the gold. She was its movement. She and the locket were one.

How long she remained in that other world she did not know but suddenly breaking through like waves on a rocky shore she heard the deep vibrations of: "*Om Om.Om Om Om.Om*" Then the fakir spoke: "*All will be well for you, Memsahib. Walk on.*"

With that he handed back the locket, and staring straight ahead, his two pupils rose upwards and slid behind his eyelids. He had moved on but his body remained.

The woman, dazed, shaken, and now shivering despite the heat, stared at him without seeing, lurched away and began to walk unsteadily back towards the train.

After her husband had spoken to her - she knew he must have done because she had dimly heard her name "*Violet*" - she remained with her eyes closed, swaying gently with the movement of the railway carriage.

A thought exploded into her mind. Her eyes flicked wide open and the words: "*God. Oh my God,*" burst from her. She did not hear her husband speak.

All she could think of was that the fakir had spoken to her in Punjabi, an Indian dialect which she did not know, and she had understood him and answered in the same language.

With a shaking hand she reached up to the golden locket. Had she taken it off? Had she handed it to the fakir? Was it all a dream? But the locket was not there. "*Why are you holding the locket in your hand,*" her husband asked, good-humored. " *You want to be careful. Someone might take it.*"

I heard this story from the woman, Violet Pallister-Young, while we were walking along the beach at Devonport, near Auckland. We had been talking about divining and were lost in thoughtful silence. "*Richard, I first came across divining when I lived with my husband in India.*"

And then she related her experience with the fakir. Mrs Young and I had met in a cafe in Manners Street, Wellington where my brother and I had gone for coffee. Both of us were smokers at that time and before we lit our cigarettes my brother asked the distinguished looking woman sitting opposite if she minded whether we smoked. " *Young man,*" she said, imperiously. "*You are unusual. Most people would light their cigarettes and blow the smoke in my face.*"

And so began a long friendship between her and myself which moved from New Zealand to the Isle of Wight in the United Kingdom where for five years I stayed with her whenever my work as a journalist permitted.

Why the subject of divining had cropped up I can't remember but Mrs Young and I covered so many different subjects that I suppose it was inevitable I would raise it because divining had become inextricably woven into of my life. Mrs Young and I met many times in New Zealand as I was a seaman on a run from Auckland-Sydney-Kure, in Japan and back to Auckland.

68

When I arrived back on one trip I rang her hotel but she had left. I dropped a line to her care of her bank saying I was shipping out to Southampton and you can imagine my surprise when, on arrival, I received a reply saying: *"I'm back home at Shanklin. Please come and see me."*

My relationship with Mrs Young developed into an intimate if unusual friendship. She was well into her 60s while I was 23. Sometimes I wondered if we could read each others minds as during the many hours we spent together we always seemed to know what the other was thinking. This is very rare even with people of the same generation.

Mrs Young - I never called her anything else other than by her surname and often I wondered why. Perhaps it illustrated a basic respect I had for her age and for herself as a person.

During the next five years I learned much about her, including that she was born into a very wealthy family whose fortune was tied up in industry. Educated at Roedene, one of Britain's most exclusive girls' public schools, she received a BA in history at Oxford and later made her debut when King George V and Queen Mary introduced young women of the upper class into society at *"Coming-out"* balls at Buckingham Palace. She married while young to a rising young British Colonial Office official who later become a top executive in the Indian railway company.

Mrs Young was one of the fortunate women who spent the winter months in India then returned to Europe before the June monsoons began. Without children, her life revolved around society functions many of which were held at her beautiful home in the exclusive French Cote D'Argent town town of Biarritz, near the Spanish border. For many years her life was posh (port out, standard board home) until just before the war when her husband was transferred to a position in South Africa railways, where he died. She was on a world tour when we met in New Zealand.

In South Africa Mrs Young had come across a diviner who was employed by a prospecting company to find gold, which he did with a pendulum. This man had the ability to locate gold deep within the earth, including both gold nuggets and reefs.

In fact the man claimed he could "*almost see*" the gold reefs in the ground. It was Mrs Young's descriptions of this man that encouraged me to try so hard to find gold later in Bendigo.

On one of my visits to Shanklin, Mrs Young, who was learning to paint miniature portraits, asked me whether a certain painting in a book was by Rubens or of one the Rubens schools.

I had done a few paintings of Australian gumtrees and cowsheds before swapping my brushes for a passport and portmanteau, but the Rubens era was the next grade up. I told her: "*I'm afraid I haven't got a clue.*"

Without looking up she said: "*Use your pendulum.*" I had read of the French priest, the Abbe Mermet, identifying substances by pendulum counts, a method which he used also to assess the artistic abilities of musical composers.

I pulled out a small pendulum I always carried and held it over the photograph in question. The pendulum oscillated 41 times then gyrated the same number of times. I then held the pendulum over a photograph of Ruben's famous painting Woman in a Fur Coat and the count was the same.

This was an exciting result as it could mean that it was possible to identify whether a painting was authentic or not.
Next I held the pendulum over Rubens' brilliant painting of Thomas Howard, the 2nd Earl of Arundel, and again got a reading of 41.

Delving into Mrs Young's library I was soon surrounded with a stack of art books and here is the list of some of the counts I drew up:

Rubens	41
Caravaggio	70
Passignano	42
Titian	72
Bernini	69
Rodin	6
David	50

Here are three counts for Australian painters which, perhaps, diviners might like to enlarge.

Arthur Boyd	9
Drysdale	28
Dobell	31

This is an area which could be investigated to ascertain whether the number of counts is linked with creative ability. The Abbe Mermet devised a system for rating the ability and creativity of musicians but he never explained how he did it.

Mrs Young had a particular disliking for Germans, whom she always referred to in scathing tones as "*The Boche*". We had many arguments about this but her prejudice remained unshaken.

As an Australian, too young to have been touched by the war and by nature an idealist, I believed there were good and bad people in every nationality including my own.

One night we were consuming martinis at an increasingly fast rate as our argument over this hotted up. Suddenly there was a long silence.

" *You don't understand, Richard,*" she said. " *Yes I am prejudiced. I hate them. I was in France when the Vichy Government under Marshall Petain gave two-thirds of France to Germany. Only a fool didn't realise that Petain's collaborator, Pierre Laval, was going to hand the South of France over to Hitler as well, so I joined the French Resistance.*

As I spoke fluent colloquial French I was given the job of dispensing petrol at a garage where I was to identify German infiltrators and saboteurs. Early one morning an old Citreon car pulled up and a haggard young Frenchman got out.

Bearded and unwashed he staggered over to me and said his wife was in the back seat of the car but he couldn't get her to move. She had been in the back seat for three weeks while he had zigzagged his way south first through occupied France then down the coast road through Bordeaux to Berlin where I was working.

The back of the car was riddled with bullet holes, and nothing remained of the rear or side windows. I opened the door and the stink that hit me was incredible, utterly impossible to describe. His wife had not left the car to go to the toilet for the whole three weeks. In her arms she held a bundle from which oozed green liquid. The driver gasped:

"The Boche machine gunned the car and killed the baby and now she won't let it go."

Between us we pulled the woman from the car and while the husband held her I jerked the putrid bundle from her arms. She began screaming, the guttural bellowing of a demented animal which she kept up until I yelled at him: 'For God's sake, hit her.' He hit her with his fist and she fell unconscious where she lay, foam dribbling from her mouth onto the cobblestones. I took the bundle around the back of the garage and buried it. I still wake at night with that screaming in my ears and the stench in my nose.

Mrs Young was clutching the wineglass so tightly it crushed in her hand, cutting one finger. As I was binding it up with my handkerchief she wiped away a tear.

After the war Mrs Young returned to Biarritz to find that the Gestapo had used her home as its local headquarters.

> *"The wonderful timber floors had been scarred by their jackboots, some of the Louis 16th paneling had been splintered, the balustrading removed, and all but one Louis chair had disappeared,"* she said. *"I stayed at an hotel where I had many reunions with local residents and I debated what to do about the house. It could have been refurbished but I had no heart for the job as it represented so much of my life which had passed and locally it linked with so much tragedy and despair."*

Finally, Mrs Young had workmen remove the remainder of the panelling and ship it to the Isle of Wight where her family had always lived. There she found an old stone stable, originally part of a mansion, and used the panelling to transform it into the beautiful home in which she now lived.

It always seems incredible to me how one part of one's life repeats itself in different forms and at different times as if waiting for your personal recognition and development. During the years I knew Mrs Young the subject of divining came up many times in our conversations.

Mrs Young said that on one of her home visits from India she became ill and after the family doctor could not diagnose the cause, she was referred to a Harley Street physician.

"He was a small man, white-haired and bearded and with a charming smile," she said. *"But when he began examining me his face was transformed by his intense concentration to such an extent that he seemed to become another person."*

Mrs Young said that eventually the doctor told her he believed the problem lay in her bile duct, a minor problem which could be relieved by medication. And then he startled her by asking if she would mind his trying a rather unusual method of diagnosis. With her keen interest in anything new, Mrs Young agreed whereupon the doctor removed a small crystal pendulum from his waistcoat pocket and held it in front of her. *"It was an incredible moment,"* she said. *"Into my mind flashed the picture of the fakir under the banyan tree at Bhatinda."*

She said that as with the fakir the pendulum began to gyrate in small circles which grew larger until they were about three inches in diameter, about the length of the small silver chain on which the crystal was suspended.

After a moment the doctor put the pendulum back in his pocket and told her that he had confirmed his diagnosis and the appropriateness of the medication he was about to prescribe. She said the doctor glanced at her quizzically, obviously to see her reaction and it was then she told him about the fakir. I asked Mrs Young what effect his treatment had on her.

"Oh, I had no further trouble," she replied. Later I was to read in Christopher's Bird's book that a Harley Street physician, Dr Aubrey Westlake, had been a pioneer member of the Medical Society for the Study of Radiesthesia (the French name for divining). I was amazed to read his list of qualifications - BA, MB, Chir.(Cantab), MRCS, LRCP, FI Psi M. I wonder if he were Mrs Young's physician.

One day when we were walking in her garden discussing something or other, she noticed a rosebush whose leaves were tinged with yellow. *"Button,"* she called.

Within a minute her gardener appeared, rake in one hand, cap in the other. The man actually touched his forelock, a salute I'd read about but never actually seen. I'd always believed it a subservient gesture which had died in Dickensian times.

"Button," said Mrs Young, imperiously, *"What have you done to that rose. It's dying."* The poor man looked as dejected as the rose. *"It's a yellowin, ma'am,"* he replied disconsolately. *"You'd better do something about it, Button,"* Mrs Young said with a glare.

We left poor Button gazing reflectively from the rose to a pile of horse manure in the corner of the garden. Back in her study she told me that once in a garden adjoining a French vineyard she had seen an elderly woman hold a small pendulum over a withered shrub and as she began to mumble the pendulum began to move.

She was told that the woman was trying to establish the cause of the plant's deterioration. She said she was assured that in the hands of certain people the practice worked, just as it did with diagnosing the illnesses of animals.

Later in Christopher Bird's book *"Divining"* I saw a photograph of a French veterinarian holding a pendulum over the withers of a draught horse and read that the use of pendulum in veterinary diagnosis had become quite common.

On returning to the house I tackled Mrs Young over the way she had addressed her gardener. With the brashness of youth coupled with the independence typical of antipodeans, I raised the matter.*"You are wrong to talk to that man you way you did,"* I said. *"He is a human being and as such is person of dignity. Also he has a title, Mister, which should be accorded to him by everyone, including his employer."*

Them was fightin' words and a three-martini argument waxed hot and strong. Suddenly there was silence as Mrs Young stared at a corner of a rug on the polished floor. *"You know, Richard,"* she said. *"We British failed in India because we considered we were better than the Indians and that it was our right to rob them. It was no wonder they mutinied, and made a saint out of Ghandi who led them towards independence. And here I am back in the Isle of Wight treating my own servant as we treated the Indians."*

I shall always remember her for that statement for it showed both the measure of her intelligence, her remorse and her ability to adjust to change. With that fierce look of determination which I knew so well, she jabbed at the button on her desk. Seconds later there was a knock at the door and in shuffled the gardener, cap in hand, and with apprehension on his face. *"Button,"* she said. *"Richard has just said I was belittling you by calling you 'Button.' Henceforth you will be known as 'Mr Button.' That's all, Mr Button. You can go back to my roses"*.

I thought it politic not to smile, but I would have loved to have heard the ensuing conversation between Mr Button and his wife, who was the housekeeper.

As a young man I suffered badly with acne and my back and neck is covered with the scars. On one ship I had several carbuncles across my shoulders, and during an inspection, the chief officer found me lying face down in my bunk. *"Go into the galley and peel some spuds,"* he growled. *"A bit of work will take your mind off it."*

A masculine Mother Teresa! When I arrived in England acne spots still appeared much to my embarrassment, and one evening when I was sitting with Mrs Young in her study she remarked on my problem. *"Richard. I notice you have acne,"* she said. *"Do you realise that sex is very good for acne. It gets the blood flowing."*

I'd heard of many cures in my life, even baking an apple with its centre filled with plug tobacco and clamping it to an acne spot, but her suggestion was new. The subject was dropped but as I was beginning to know Mrs Young I wondered what she was planning.

Some weeks later I called into Shanklin as I was down that way on a job, and she told me she had arranged for me to go to a house warming party in Kensington where "*two nice clean girls*" were setting up house after making their debut.

Eventually I went to the party which was in a large upstairs flat around which were dotted small groups whose stiff postures, stilted conversation and forced laughter betrayed their nervous efforts to appear sophisticated. The two hostesses, circulated like wanding electrons, handing out "*nibbles*" and refills.

I was landed with an imposing young fellow at least six feet taller than me, dressed in black coat, striped trousers and whose stiff white collar kept his chin at a guardsman's angle. "*What do you do for a crust,*" I asked him to break through the pack ice.

"*Arm with the Forrin Orfice,*" he replied, staring at a chandelier. I was about to reply that I'd just been sacked from Fleet Street, but didn't think this would have rated highly as a conversational riposte. I moved on until standing near a group when I heard my name mentioned.

> "*Have you met that dreadful Orstralian fella. Yuh should hear his accent. Quite uncouth.*"

With my self-confidence now at shoe level (one of mine actually had a hole in the sole stuffed with paper) I quietly got my coat and retreated to a nearby pub. I didn't need a pendulum to realise I would have to become a lot more couth before I'd be invited to meet any more '*nice clean girls.*'

As I obviously was badly in need of a beautician, it was inevitable my diet should arise. I asked Mrs Young if she thought a pendulum could help a person decide on a healthy diet.

"Why not?" she replied. *"Divining is used for most purposes so what not as an aid in choosing the right foods to eat"*.

I'm afraid my knowledge of nutrition at the time could have been classified as abysmal to almost nil, and like the majority of people I really did not begin to take much interest in it until I'd turned 40 when my energy output and the mirror reflection gave me the thumbs down.

Finally at the age of 60 after several heart attacks and open-heart surgery I really got down to work on a detailed analysis of what I could and should eat and which were the big no-nos.

An excellent starting point for any diet is that suggested by the National Heart Foundation of Australia but this deals largely with main categories of foods and does not cover some of the exotic foods which may or may not be good for a person. A little uncertainly I began to go through the list of recommended foods and found my pendulum gyrated over most of them. Turning to an ordinary recipe book I did the same thing and was surprised to find that the items eschewed by the Heart Foundation the pendulum gyrated strongly in a negative direction.

Since then I use a pendulum in food selection as a matter of course. I have found it particularly handy for assessing the quality of foods which have been stored for some time in the refrigerator. I'm one of those people who wrap up left-overs in plastic, put them in the fridge and then forget what they are and how long they've been hiding at the back of a shelf. I've been very wary about cheese as when I first arrived in England in 1949 I dug into a tin of cheese I'd brought with me from New Zealand and in the morning found it was covered in green slime. A touch-and-go bout of paratyphoid followed. Of course, like most people, I turn a blind eye to certain items which the foundation is not too keen on. One is home-brewed beer, which David Horsfall introduced me to (I have to blame someone).

David, who is noted for his poker face, once told a group of journalists, who were discussing this vitally important subject, that unless he had about 500 bottles of home brew in his garage he felt his security was beginning to erode. An awed silence followed. Naturally, both of us now being skilled brewers we are able to moderate the alcohol content of our vintages. While each prefers a different style of beer, we both concur that brew testing time is a noble and worthy occasion.

Eventually I lost contact with Mrs Young. I found a long suffering English girl who was able to put up with my strange Australian attitudes and we got married. Mrs Young was one of the witnesses at the ceremony. We wrote a few times but inevitably and also sadly the years intervened. And then my letters were returned marked "*Not known at this address.*"

Divining in Tasmania

The late Geoff. Little, of Burnie, was well known throughout Northern Tasmania as capable water diviner. His widow, Mrs Bromley Little, said he used mainly a cane rod or an angled wire. She said;

> "*Practically all his efforts were able to be drilled on and produced bore water in usable quantities for irrigation,*"

One opal rare, please......

Divining for opals on a Central Victorian football ground might sound like looking for ice cream in the Sahara Desert, but the centre of the Kennington Oval near Bendigo was the scene of a prolonged series of experiments trying to establish whether opals could be located with an L-wire or pendulum.

Opal mining is such a haphazard business that a person can spend a lifetime of money and energy searching for the gems and miss a fortune by a fraction of an inch. So to find any means by which the search could be made more accurate would be like manna from heaven for work-weary opal miners.

A visit to any of Australia's opal fields, most of which have become moonscapes of abandoned mineshafts and mullock heaps, is eloquent testimony to the need for a more precise means of locating these precious gems.

It was the Japanese predilection for opals which introduced me to the gems described by the Australian gemstone expert Frank Leechman as; *"beautiful, fascinating, mysterious....... a peerless Queen of Gems which defies imitation."*

What more could I add. I was working for the Australian Dairy Board in Melbourne at the time trying to flog a bit of cheese when the chairman called me into his office and asked me what I knew about opals. As a good journalist is supposed to be a walking encyclopedia, I gave him the standard *"A-little-bit"* type of answer and waited to do a quick mental entrechat to get out of trouble. It appeared that a group of top-brass Japanese dairy food importers, accompanied by their wives, were hitting the town and the boss felt obliged to throw on a barbie along with the odd gift as a sweetener.

Now I was ok with a bit of damper with a side serve of roast goanna, but somehow I didn't think he had this in mind, especially when he wanted opals as gifts rather than those other priceless Australian gems: icy cans of Fosters.

However an inspired thought, a process which often got me out of trouble (and into it on more than one occasion) brought forth the name of Vincent Rosales, the gastronomic maestro whose restaurant is in Toorak Road, South Yarra.

After I retreated to my office to ponder the boss's orders I did what journalists the world over do when it doubt - reach for the telephone directory. A blur of yellow pages and - Ah! there was in big bold letters - Maxim's, Toorak Road, South Yarra; phone: 866 5500. A wiggle with a finger and Vincent's rich, baritone voice answered. I was saved by the skin of a pickled onion. He said; "*Of course I can help, Richard, just tell me how many guests and leave everything to me.*"

When you give a "*money-no-object*" order to Maxim's, the equivalent of the world's best cuisine is assured. Not for nothing did this epicurean entrepreneur name his restaurant after world-famous Maxim's, of Paris, a fact acknowledged by the glitterati of famous bon viveurs who equate not dining at Vincent's Maxim's as not having visited Melbourne.

Royalty of all levels, heads of state of every nationality, captains of commerce and industry, the intelligentsia, military leaders, politicians, and of course a few hoi poloi like myself have all been Vincent's guests. One of the oddities of his restaurant is the mixed decor, ranging from rare paintings and vases to comparatively cheap baroque Victorian mirrors and all stops in between. Vincent explains it this way: "*In Melbourne, especially in Toorak and South Yarra, patrons have come to regard Maxim's as an extension of their own homes, and when a guest whom I have known for years presents me with some article from their home as a token of their affection and appreciation I am genuinely touched and it would be most hurtful to decline the gift."*

My boss's instructions about the menu included one item which caused a big hiccup in planning of this lavish dinner. It had to include avocados whose bland, subtle taste is guaranteed to send Japanese taste buds into paroxysms of delight.

The trouble was avocados were not in season. Vincent and I commenced a *'Holy-Grail'* search of Melbourne and Sydney for a box of avocados, frantically phoning wholesalers, distributors and retailers but the result was negative. The Victorian Wholesale Market said one box of the exotic fruit had arrived from interstate but no one knew who had bought it. So Vincent and I rang all the leading hotels and restaurants but the box had disappeared into Melbourne's culinary maw.

However Vincent, never fazed by such a minor problem, produced an alternative entree which red-carpeted the fabulous main meal. When I saw the embossed menu with its ladder of succulent delicacies, I reluctantly had to admit it rather outshone my rabbit-on-a-shovel suggestions. If I remember correctly it ran something like the chart opposite.

Then came the question of gifts. The boss had said it had to be opal cufflinks for the men, as Japanese businessmen prized them, and opal pendants and baby koalas for their wives which would bring a similar sparkle to their eyes.

A regular bushman at heart I knew the difference between a koala and a wombat, and soon found a line of soft, cuddly items made from best bunny fur. But with the opals I was in uncharted waters. A quick dash back to my reference library and I found a list of jewellers who specialised in them and my precious gemstone education began.

MENU

Entree
Prawns Maxim's - Panfried Prawns flambeed in brandy
blended in a lobster cream sauce topped with hollandaise
sauce.

Main
Duckling a L'Orange - Boneless Crisp Roasted Half
duckling carved, on a Grand Marnier sauce & accompanied
with orange segments.

Dessert
Maxim's Famous Chocolate Souffle - served with Praline Ice
Cream.

Cafe
Cafe Noir & Maxim's home made Petits Fours

At every shop there were glass cases and trays of scintillating
arrays of opals and opal jewellery from all the famous opal
fields of Australia - Queensland, New South Wales and South
Australia and they were in all sizes, shapes, colours and
settings.

I quickly learned the difference between solid opal, doublets
which were slivers of opal stuck to a hard backing, and triplets
where the doublet was covered with layer of crystal which both
enhanced and protected the gemstone.

Not knowing how much the boss wanted to spend of the dairy
farmers' money I asked a wholesaler to bring a case full of his
goodies back to the board where the boss, bless his generous
heart, took great delight in making his own selections.

The banquet in Maxim's Long Room was a tribute to Vincent's epicurean art and from the ecstatic report from the boss the food would have won a gold medal at the Chefs' Olympics. Vincent had even decorated the table setting with miniature Japanese and Australian flags.

On the side plates of the men were the jewellery boxes containing the cufflinks - all triplets - and sitting on the side-plates of the women were the little koalas each with a glistening pendant around its neck.

I didn't like to ask if the magnificent food, artistic presentation, renowned venue and half the output of Lightning Ridge sold a pound or two of butter (there are times when it's better to be discreet when you are an employee) but I gained two things from the exercise - a lasting friendship with Vincent and a deep appreciation of the beauty of Australian opals.

Before leaving the comfort of Maxim's for wind-swept Kennington football ground, readers may be interested to know how the restaurant came to exist in Melbourne.

The story began when a young Spaniard who wanted to reach Australia, stowed away on an Argentinian training ship, La Argentina, when it visited the Spanish port of Cadiz in 1947. His name was Vincent Rosalles. He and two friends hid in the engine-room without food or water until they were discovered three days later and hauled before the captain. Vincent, suffering from dysentery, was put in the ship's hospital.

The trio were put ashore in the Canary Islands and two months later returned to Spain. So determined was he to reach Australia Vincent stowed away on two more ships before eventually reaching Sydney where he "*jumped ship*" during the New Year's Day celebrations in 1948. Eventually the Australian immigration authorities granted him citizenship.

A delightful irony is that later when La Argentina, visited Melbourne, the master, Capt.Pedro Onevi, who was the executive officer on the vessel when Vincent stowed away on it, was taken to dine at Maxim's as the guest of the Argentine Consul.

When Vincent welcomed his guests, he and the captain stared at each other in surprise. The long moment was broken when Capt.Onevi put out his hand, and a friendship was renewed.

Several years later when I was surveying a Wedderburn mine for "*Robbie*" Robertson, of Kangaroo Flat, he mentioned that a former mate of his had gone opal mining at Lightning Ridge in New South Wales. "*Have you ever tried to divining for opals?*" he asked, as he added another shovelful to the rising mullock heap beside his mine.

Frankly I'd never thought of doing this but on the 60-kilometre drive back to Bendigo I began wondering if a diviner would react to opals. First step was to learn about the composition of opals so I stopped off at the Bendigo public library, selected an opus or two on the subject, and retired to my armchair at home to bone up on the subject.

With an iced stubby for company, I began flipping through the wonderful collection of photographs of flashing, iridescent opals found in Australia and read about their chemical composition, discovery, mining, marketing and the folk law that had grown up around them.

Apparently a Queensland opal field was discovered accidentally in 1901 when a stampeding bullock kicked over a stone which flashed in the sunlight. The stockman chasing the bullock, Englishman Clement Tyrrell, dismounted and picked up the stone the underside of which revealed an opal about 5 cm long.

He gave the opal, described as showing the "*blended fire of ruby, topaz, emerald and sapphire,*" to the daughter of his employer. Tyrrell named the bullock *"Opal"* and returned it to the herd instead of having it sold for slaughter.

The Japanese dinner at Maxim's had introduced me to the uniqueness of the black fire opal found at Lightning Ridge in Northern New South Wales but its value came as a shock. It was regarded as the best in the world and huge prices were being paid for even small stones. *"Precious opal is a non-crystalline form of silica and its chemical formula is $SiO_2\, nH_2O$,"* stated in one book. Being a diviner who had cut his baby teeth on looking for groundwater, the H_2O indicated that opal contained water which apparently varied from 2 to 13 percent. The iridescent fire of black opal came from light reflecting and refracting from thin veins of water locked within the matrix of potch, a semi-transparent, solidified, valueless jelly prevalent in opal country.

Next I contacted the Bendigo Gem Club where a generous member gave me a bag of potch, some of which contained flashes of opal but none large enough to grind down into a gemstone. However I was able to find one irregular sliver large enough to act as a divining test sample.

Experiments in the living room of my home and on the front lawn revealed that opals radiated an energy ring similar to electromagnetic rings which radiate from a wire when current surges through it.

However in the case of opals the radiation was spherical and so could be detected from above as well as from the sides. This energy ring varied in diameter according to the size of the opal.

Robbie helped me with the field testing at Kennington oval. While I was out of sight around a corner he would hide the opal somewhere on the surface of the oval. Ten minutes later I would begin walking across the oval until the L-wire indicated I had crossed an energy line.

Next step was to mark the arc of the energy line on the ground. When I had found a significant arc I would drive pegs into each end then run a string between them making a chord across the arc. Exactly half way along this chord I would drive in another peg and then, using a compass, sight a line at 90 degrees from it in the direction of the centre of the circle of which the arc was part of the circumference.

I would walk along this sighted line until the L-wire swung sideways which indicated the wire was directly over the opal. We repeated this experiment until we were confident an opal could be found quickly and accurately by this means.

Next we tackled the problem of depthing an opal in the ground, not an easy task. However we found that the same method of locating opals horizontally also applied to finding them vertically.

Our depthing experiments involved placing the opal at the base of a 2 metre high fence then raising a small pendulum vertically until it reacted to the opal's energy ring. We would then follow the ring both sides until it reached the ground at which points we drove in pegs thereby establishing the opal's chord.

Here we faced a mathematical problem - knowing the height of the arc and its length, was it possible using geometry to calculate the centre of the circle, the source of the energy ring. This was solved by Kevin Daw, of the Applied Science Department of the Victorian Institute of tafe, Bendigo, who gave us the formula:

$$\mathbf{R} = \frac{X2 + Y2}{2Y2}$$

To the algebraic illiterate such as myself the sight of these figures caused an immediate mental blockage. However their application did not prove difficult as Appendix 5, demonstrates.

This might seem an involved way of locating opals and I am certain that in the field it could be short-circuited by simply using the L-wire as a pointer to locate an opal horizontally. But when it comes to depthing, the pointing method will not work and a diviner would have to rely on the question-and-answer system of using a pendulum, a doubtful procedure when emotionally involved in the outcome. I pursued solving the problem mathematically so it could be used in remote map divining, which I believe can be used in all stages of opal mining, especially in the re-examination of old abandoned workings where it is quite likely large pockets of opal could have been missed by only a few centimetres.

Obtaining a map of the Lightning Ridge opal field I surveyed it remotely and believe there are at least three areas where undiscovered loads of rich opal exist. Also I believe that using this method it should be possible to go carefully through old abandoned workings and ascertain if the old diggers have missed any pockets of opals.

All opal miners know that an opal can be covered by a millimetre of dirt and miss the probing of their picks. It may seem to some readers that the introduction of mathematics into the divining for opals is a trifle exotic but when it comes to remote map divining the necessity to be precise is paramount.

The results of my experiments in evolving a mathematical approach to finding opals are detailed in Appendix 5.

As the reader will understand my involvement with opals will always be associated with my friendship with Vincent Rosales and that magnificent banquet given for the Japanese visitors his restaurant in South Yarra.

If anyone is tempted to try a similar repast then all they have to do is dial (03) 866 5500. If you are ever in Paris then you should visit Maxim's Restaurant, 3 Rue Royale (Phone: (1) 42 65 27), to get an idea of what Vincent can offer you.

Dogged by error

I love dogs, especially my little dog, Tiny, a cross Corgi-Jack Russell, which I reared from 10 days of age. An itinerant citrus picker, moving on from Mildura, in North-West Victoria, had broken the necks of five pups when I intervened. "Take it or it's gone," he said. So I took it - a tiny handful of wriggling fur with beady eyes and a pointy nose. She was eight in 1990 when I had to leave Newbridge, west of Bendigo in North-Central Victoria, because of heart disease. I gave Tiny to an elderly neighbour who loved her. Recently I learned she had gone blind but was still happily pottering around her garden.

Hearing of a greyhound breeder near Bendigo I visited his kennels, where, at his request, I ran my pendulum over his latest litter. To awed onlookers I pronounced one dog superior to the others.

The owner, Cliff Garland, informed me later that the pup grew into an excellent specimen and was snapped up by another greyhound racer. I felt pretty smug until he reported that the dog's testicles had grown so big they rubbed on the inside of its legs, and had to be removed. Another divining error.

Recently when editing a book on donkeys I came on the word "entire." The local vet. said it meant a jack which had not been castrated, adding: "*Testic*les are a nasty word to horsey people. That means you and I are entire," I said. "*speak for yourself,*" he replied.

The great south land

The towering cliffs and jagged reefs along the western coast of Victoria from Cape Otway to the South Australian border are a fearsome spectacle from the sea.

Geologically the coast is largely sedimentary having been the floor of the Southern Ocean until violent volcanic convulsions thrust it upward, injecting vents of magma to form the ferocious claws at its feet poised to rip the hull of any ship off course or trapped by wind or tide.

Over the past 200 years this has been the graveyard of hundreds of ships, and seafarers have given it the grim title of *"The Shipwreck Coast."* The history of the Shipwreck Coast began several centuries before the mapping of the eastern coastline of Australia by Captain James Cook.

There are legends of exploration of the Great South Land, as Australia was known, by ocean-going Chinese junks which regularly made trading voyages along South-East Asian coastlines.

As Northern Australia is just over 500 kilometres from the island of Timor, it is not unreasonable to think that the Chinese ventured that last distance to the Australian mainland.

Undoubtedly they would have heard of the many voyages of local fishermen who reaped rich harvests of shellfish from Bathurst Island to the Bonaparte Archipelago.

At that time European seamen were also coast huggers, lacking the means of accurate offshore navigation rather than courage. Fired by the Atlantic voyages of the former Italian pirate, Christopher Columbus, which were financed by Spain, the other great maritime nation, Portugal, began the exploration of the coast of Africa.

The goal was to achieve a sea route to the spice islands of the Far East which had been discovered by the Portuguese explorer, Ferdinand Magellan, in 1516. Using a flat-earth navogational system of sailing due south to a certain latitude and then due east until they hit the coast, they eventually turned east at the Cape of Good Hope and proceeded by the same triangular system to South-East Asia where they established a trading and ship-repair outpost on Timor, which was to last for 400 years.

In 1529, at the end of their seven-year war, Portugal and Spain signed a treaty which divided the world in half, with the antipodean dividing line being the present West Australian-South Australian border.

Later Portugal paid Spain 300,000 ducats to shift the border 17 degrees farther east, which means that Victoria's Shipwreck Coast now belonged to Portugal, giving it exploration rights.

While Portugal punctiliously avoided exploring east of this new demarcation line - for to do so could have re-ignited the war - evidence exists that they did undertake secret explorations of the forbidden eastern coast.

These were led by Gnomes de Sequeira and Cristovao de Mendonca both of whom were sworn to secrecy and whose maps were sent back to Lisbon. The evidence of their explorations is the Dauphin Map published in 1536, the details of which are believed to have been leaked from Portugal's maritime archives.

As the coastline shown on this map ended near Warrnambool this is reasonable proof that at least one of these Portuguese expeditions reached this point, otherwise why should it been on the map? At first glance the Dauphin Map, which labels Australia as Jave La Grande, bears little relationship with current maps of Australia. This is not surprising considering that it was made from plain geometrical observations of latitude and bearing.

In his fascinating book *The Secret Discovery of Australia*, Ken McIntyre, the world-acclaimed researcher of Portuguese maritime history, relates how *"by good luck"* he solved the mystery of the Dauphin Map's distortions by converting its cartographic points to spherical geometry, a reconstruction which gave Australia something akin to its present outline.

Time warp takes us to 1836 when a very minor shipwreck occurred, the overturning of a small whale boat near estuary of the Hopkins River at Warrnambool. The boat commander, Captain Smith, who was in charge of the whaling station at Port Fairy, some 26 kilometres farther west, was drowned but his crew, named Watson and Gibbs, swam ashore and had to walk back along the coast. An official report made at the time states that on this journey they found the wreck of a vessel, which they said looked to be of Spanish origin.

Later the Port Fairy habor master, Captain Mills, visited the wreck and took bearings of it from a nearby Tower Hill. In the years following there were many reports of local people seeing the wreck, even from those who played on it as children, but eventually the last of its ribs and keel were swallowed by drifting sand dunes.

Later research gave strength to the wreck being Portuguese as descriptions of the timber used in its construction were similar to that used for ship construction in Timor. Also the carvel method of planking - butting one plank against another rather than overlapping them - was used in Portuguese ships.

Early reports that the deck planks had both the texture and hardness of mahogany eventually led to the name "*The Mahogany Ship*" being given to the wreck and this has now become part of local folklore. The principal reason for the wreck achieving its present-day fame is that historians believe it could identify which country, in fact, did discover Australia.

Over the years many searches have been made of the area but no evidence of the wreck has been found. Several years ago the Victorian Government offered a reward of $250,00 for its discovery but although scientists, equipped with the latest electronic equipment, made a most thorough survey, which was called "*Operation Sandfly*," nothing was found. Many diviners, no doubt encouraged by the rich reward, have tried to locate the Mahogany Ship but without success.

The most recent search was made by a diviner, who claimed he had found the wreck using a hand-held wood saw. Apparently the saw - which he had selected because of its flexibility and resonance - had wobbled convincingly over a spot in a coastal car park but a hole drilled where he indicated was unsuccessful. Decayed wood retrieved from the hole was found to be of a species of pine tree, similar to the famous Huon Pine of Western Tasmania.

After a series of reports in the local paper about being on the verge of finding the wreck he was forced to abandon the search. Living at Port Fairy at the time and being a diviner I followed the progress of this search with keen interest and even went over the site. I agree that it was the site of a wreck at one time but the shape obtained by pendulum movements, seemed more like a Chinese junk than a lateen-rigged caravel. However there was no acceptable evidence of this.

At the time I had become friends with a retired company director, Tony Foster, who lived some 220 kilometres away at Mt Macedon, some 65 kilometres north-west of Melbourne.

I had given him full details of the Mahogany Ship, obtained from a special committee in Warrnambool set up to co-ordinate the various searches which were going on at the time. One Saturday afternoon the phone rang and it was Tony. He said, *"I've read all the stuff you sent me and have just being going over an ordinary road map showing the Warrnambool-Port Fairy coast and I've got a strong reaction on the beach near Killarney between the two towns. Would you like to check it out for me please?"*

Tony had proven his skill as a map diviner so I had no hesitation in doing what he asked. I had survey maps of the beach at Killarney so I commenced a pendulum search of the area.

At precisely the place he had nominated I too got a strong reaction but what it was I had no idea. Although the weather was pretty dirty as it so often is along that coast, I set off by car and eventually reached the target area.

Because the wind was gusting spitefully I found that my L-wire was difficult to read so I resorted to a large lead fishing weight on the end of stout cord.

I didn't find anything for the first 60 metres when suddenly the pendulum, which I had made to oscillate in the direction I was walking, switched to a vigorous sideways movement against the wind. I marked the place on the sand with a stick and then approached it from the opposite direction. The same reaction occurred but this time some 10 metres from the first line.

The wind dropped and I was able to use a smaller pendulum and to my amazement the shape I then marked out began to resemble the keel or keelson of a vessel about 30 - 40 metres in length with a beam of about 0.8 metres. The remains of ribs at uniform distances of about one metre were clearly defined.

If this wasn't an interesting enough discovery, then the next shape identified had me standing there in such excitement that I was oblivious to the rain which had begun to fall. I had marked out a shape in the sand to the left side of the hull but could not identify it. It resembled a large box like an over-sized coffin, and even tapered towards one end like a coffin.

Getting down on my hands and knees I began tracing the outline more accurately and to my astonishment it began to resemble a small canon. With my usual scepticism I began to look for proof such as the touch hole and soon found it. Continuing to trace the outline with great care I found outlines of projections on either side. These were about the diameter and length of the shafts by which a cannon is elevated and depressed on its carriage. The mouth of the cannon seemed to have a ring-like bulge around it which was puzzling, but later I inspected similar cannon at the Port Fairy's Battery Park and I found the bulge was re-inforcing at the muzzle end.

I phoned Tony with details of my survey findings and he said: *"That's just about what I've got on a scaled drawing I've just completed."*

I spent the next few days exploring the site and accurately mapping by triangulation every point at which my pendulum reacted. I laid a large sheet of heavy paper over the canon markings and holding this in place with stones, copied them with a felt pen. Later I spread the paper out on the living room floor and using a small pendulum corrected errors caused at the beach by the wind and the lumpy sand under the paper. I posted this drawing to Tony who confirmed its accuracy.

One interesting reaction in the sand was in the shape of three coins. Later I drew these up to a very large scale - about 1 cm to 15 cms - and was able to pick out some strange markings which resembled parts of letters.

Portuguese Caravels

I showed this drawing to a friend whose hobby was numismatics, and he said the marks appeared to be like those on some early Portuguese coins but he was unable to make a positive identification. Eventually Tony came down to Port Fairy for the weekend and surveyed the site himself. Although we differed in minor details our overall results were the same.

A word must be said here about Tony's and my relationship as diviners. As a person he is extremely practical and pursues problems relentlessly until they are solved. This is undoubtedly one of the reasons he was such a success in industry. We do not always accept each other divining results but over what we had found at Killarney Beach we are in close agreement.

The Killarney Beach is some 10 kilometres west of where the Mahogany Ship is supposed to rest, but neither Tony nor I claim to have found this vessel.

If our surveys are right then it could prove that another Portuguese vessel was wrecked in the area, or even that the traditional site nearer to Warrnambool is that of a Spanish ship. I have surveyed the whole of the coast from Warrnambool to Port Fairy and found a total of five possible sites of ancient wrecks. This is not surprising, as there must have been many more passages by explorers' vessels other than those recorded in history and quite a few could well have been claimed by that unforgiving shore. Testimony to this is the number of modern vessels equipped with sophisticated navigation equipment which have come to grief there.

While neither Tony nor I claim to have positively identified the wreck of a 16th century sailing ship by divining, our independent results and the fact that they were obtained by two people operating about 300 kilometres apart must give open-minded historians interested in establishing who discovered Australia some food for thought.

Earlier, with another diviner, I had attempted to locate the famed Mahogany Ship near Warrnambool. We did get a reading which seemed to indicate a vessel of some sort had been in the vicinity but shallow boring produced nothing which could have been subjected to carbon dating.

We used a special map divining technique, devised by this diviner, which I have applied in several investigations and can recommend it for the speedy and accurate location of a target. This is explained in Appendix 4.

The eyes have it

During my years as a scribe I had met a few New Age health workers who claimed to be able to identify illnesses by staring into people's eye but I hadn't given the practice much attention. However, some months before writing, I saw advertisements for iridology services in a reputable journal and I had wondered if the study of the eyes were now regarded by the medical profession as a legitimate diagnositic aid.

Later during a meeting with Adrian Schoo, a leading physiotherapist in Northern Victoria, the subject of iridology was raised. Adrian had rung the *Bendigo Advertiser* where I had been employed to find out if they knew of a water diviner, who had some knowledge of adverse telluric radiations. Having seen me win a bet by locating a gold-plated coin in the adjoining Court House Hotel and so win a few glasses of beer, my former colleagues nominated me as an expert.

In addition to being a qualified physiotherapist Adrian held a university degree in acupuncture, both of which callings gave him an extraordinarily deep insight into the power and workings of the mind and its ability both to cause and remedy human "*dis-ease.*" A firm believer in the negative effect of geopathetic stress on the human body Adrian wanted to know if there were any concentrations of adverse energy radiations under a housing block of land he was considering buying.

I surveyed a couple of prospective blocks for him and then, when invited to dine with him and his delightful wife, Madeleine, took the opportunity to check the rooms where they and their family slept. I was not sure whether they took kindly to my suggestion that the only safe area for them to sleep was in an attic bedroom where swinging a cat would have been exceedingly detrimental to the feline population. However on checking six months later Adrian reported: "*We are still sleeping upstairs and sleep very well.*"

Adrian visited my flat many times and in conversations which flicked from subject to subject the word iridology came up. I found he knew a lot about the subject and even had a relative who was an accomplished practitioner. Adrian lent me a book on iridology and from this I began to realise it was just as legitimate a part of medicine as acupuncture, despite the fact that some physicians would have suggested it being classified under the Dewey System as 631.86 -"*manure, agriculture for the use of.*"

However now iridology will be found in all libraries under 616.07545 - "*The identification of human physical and mental abnormalities by changes in colour, shape and formation of the irises.*"

In Europe, iridology has been developed as a valuable aid to medical diagnosis and is broadly accepted by the medical fraternity. During our conversation Adrian suggested I might like to hold a pendulum over an iridological chart to see if there were any reaction. Adopting the usual procedure I follow in remote divining I fixed my mind on a person, in this case my brother in New Zealand, and to my amazement the pendulum identified the particular ailment from which he suffers. As I had not studied the annotated charts before, I had no premature knowledge of what any area represented.

Next I tried to get a reading on my own state of health and the pendulum indicated a negative energy coming from my heart - a precise result as I had had open-heart surgery followed by a severe heart attack. With mounting interest I began a series of experiments checking the health of people whose ailments I knew about. Each time the pendulum picked out the appropriate illness or discomfort they were experiencing.

In the back of Adrian's book were blank iridological charts for both left and right eyes and turning to these I was surprised to find that when the pendulum was held over these it gyrated over the same areas as it had over the annotated charts. Both Adrian and I were excited by this discovery. Was this simply another facet of divining or was it a combination of divining and clairvoyance? We did not know. During that particular session we tried a basketful of people, some whom I knew and others who were Adrians' relatives and associates.

In all cases it appeared pendular iridological diagnosis seemed successful, however we both agreed that much more experimention was needed. Before Adrian came to see me again I went over blank charts many times and began to refine the technique. It appeared that a pendulum could pinpoint an area where negative energy was being emitted but it could not replicate the precision achievable with either the direct study of the iris or its study photographically.

While considering this finding I continued to experiment with the system and in one experiment I applied it to Adrian himself. Now, Adrian is an extremely fit person whose hobbies include marathon running and orienteering, so I approached this test prejudiced towards believing I would not get any adverse result whatsoever. However I was extremely surprised to get an indication that he had trouble with one of his eyes.

When he arrived I raised this with him and he revealed that he had been born with a cataract of the left eye. Adrian asked me about the health of his sister-in-law, Adele, who lives in Melbourne. This took our experiments into the obtuse field of having to use someone else as an intermediary, in this case Adrian, through whom I would have to make contact with the subject under consideration. Not feeling at all confident I went over the blank charts of both of Adele's eyes and rather tentatively told Adrian that they indicated she had a minor stomach problem. *"That's wrong,"* said Adrian. *"I spoke to her only a couple of days ago and she was fine."* Later he rang me and said he'd spoken with his sister-in-law again and unbeknown to him she had been to a doctor because of trouble in the precise area which my pendulum had indicated on the iridological charts.

Next day I enlarged the blank charts to A3 size and had them plasticised so that I could make felt pen marks on them which could be removed later. But the standard charts when enlarged did not seem suitable for rapid diagnosis using a pendulum. It seemed obvious I would have to design special charts. In this I was assisted by the charts devised by the natural therapies practitioner and photographic iridologist, John Friend, the author of the book, Eyes Talk, an excellent guide to iris diagnosis. Another valuable reference was. The Science and Practice of Iridology, by Dr Bernard Jensen, DC, ND.

Both Adrian and I believe that in developing a technique combining divining with iridological diagnosis, which we stumbled on quite by chance, we have achieved a world first. Adrian's comment about our experiments was: *"I think that with the help of the pendulum, your mind can pick up subtle energy differences while iridology picks up pathological changes as they take place, or can give you a general tendency towards certain diseases."*

My own attitude to combining iridology with divining does not go beyond what I achieved in my experiments - that it seems to have value as a rapid means of identifying areas of negative energy (or dis-ease as opposed to disease) in the body. Any such areas should be drawn to the attention of a qualified medical practitioner or therapist for possible confirmation and treatment. A diviner's conclusions are only a guide, and unless confirmed, should never be used as basis for any treatment of any type.

Having by now become personally convinced of the integrity of iridology, I decided to raise it when I next saw a medical specialist in Melbourne. I knew that this doctor held strictly orthodox views on medicine but nevertheless I thought his reaction would be interesting. I was not disappointed.

In between having to take deep breaths and coughing, I posed the question:*"What do you think of iridology?"* he replied *"Bullshit,"*.

This proved a point I had learned in counselling that when you ask a question which can be answered with a Yes or No it drops a kedge anchor into the conversation. Having become immune to anchors of all types being dropped on me while a newspaper reporter I continued undeterred: *"Why is it bullshit?"* *"It's more of this New Age junk being peddled by carpet-baggers,"* was the reply, which ended, *"Not worth talking about. Please open your mouth."*

A railway sleeper was thrust inside and I was asked to say: *"Ahhhh."* So ended a most enlightening dialogue.

Having drawn this prejudicial blank I decided to do some research of my own on iridology and I found it had a very ancient history. Some 3,000 year ago the Chaldeans were said to have recorded changes in the iris and their relationship to disease and injury.

In the New Testament, Luke (11:34) said: *The light of the Body is the eye: therefore when thine eye is single, thy whole body is also full of light; but when thine eye is evil, thy body also is full of darkness.*

Like many advances in science, which began by chance, the modern history of iridology began about 1860 when a Hungarian boy, Ignatz Von Peczeley, of Budapest, tried to help an owl which had broken one of its legs. Soon afterwards he noticed a dark mark appear in the lower part of the bird's eye.

He put splints on the leg and when the bone had knitted he released the bird, but strangely it chose to remain in the boy's garden as a pet.

One day young Itnatz noticed that the dark line in the bird's eyes had been replaced with a white mark. This made him wonder if the marks in the eyes were related to the broken leg and its subsequent repair. Eventually the boy became a medical doctor and while working in a Budapest hospital took the opportunity to study the eyes of people suffering from diseases and accidents. He used his observations to construct a chart of the irises on which he marked the areas which seemed to be related to the different parts of the body and their condition.

Meanwhile about the same time in Sweden, Nils Liljequist also began a similar study of irises and produced his own iridological charts. These were remarkably similar to those of Von Peczeley. Since that time iridological diagnosis has spread throughout the world and has become accepted part of natural therapies, despite the attitude of the established medical profession.

Here is how I approach an iridological study: If I do not know the subject well, I obtain a photograph of the person, or some object belonging to him or her, or if that is unavailable, I write their name on a piece of paper and place it on the blank iridology chart. If neither of these is available I concentrate on the mind of a relative or friend who knows the subject under investigation and use this link to make contact. Then concentrating on the person I am checking I hold the pendulum over the centre of the blank chart of the left eye until the pendulum begins to gyrate. This is my indication of my having established contact.

Next I ask if he or she has any source of negative vibrations emanating from their body. If there are one or more areas then the pendulum will begin changing its movement to oscillations with the direction of the swings indicating the problem areas which have to be checked later against the annotated chart. Each area is marked with a felt pen against which is noted the strength of the pendulums gyration. The diameter of gyrations appears to reflect the amount of negative energy present. The same procedure is followed on the right eye chart.

At the conclusion of the tests the two marked charts are compared with the annotated charts to ascertain what the marks mean. If the areas on the charts do not give the same readings they are ignored. The tests should be carried out each day for at least a week as it is only areas which continue to appear day after day which seem to indicate a lasting or possibly deep-seated source of negative vibrations. Practice iridological charts are in Appendix 3.

Considering the use of the pendulum in iridological diagnosis objectively, it seems to be similar to the way the pendulum is used in direct question-and-answer medical diagnosis as practiced by some leading medical practitioners, mainly in Europe, and by some Australian acupuncturists to locate the precise point for the insertion of stimulating needles. The process begs the question: Does the diviner use a pendulum over an iridological chart merely as a means of tuning into a human energy source clairvoyantly?

But then I suppose the same question could be asked of every aspect of divining.

George Murphy & Co,
water divining consultants

So reads invoices presented by George Murphy, of Albury, when he plies his trade in New South Wales, Victoria and South Australia. He says he gives a *"money-back-if-not-satisfied"* guarantee with all his work but he doesn't have to part with his fee often as in 700 divining jobs over 56 years he has had a 98 per cent success rate. He depths streams up to 150 metres and estimates bore outputs.

A new world of fossils

Today with jumbo jets, air buses and a host of other aircraft filling the skyways it is becoming difficult to remember when all international travel was by ship - only about sixty years ago. Before the Wright brothers made their historic flight at Kittyhawk in the USA, and British-born Lawrence Hargrave performed a similar feat near Sydney, in New South Wales, which is recorded on our $20 note, only birds, insects and bats were able to fly.

The largest bird was the South American vulture, the condor, whose wing-span measured 3 metres. Only some species of eagle approached this size, the biggest with a wing-span of about 2.4 metres. However, if we time-warp backwards some 190 million years to the Jurassic period when gigantic and ferocious reptiles roamed the primeval forests and plains, the largest creatures which flew were the pterodactyls, which were like huge bats. By comparison to winged creatures today they were huge, with an average wing-span of about 7.6 metres.

No fossil evidence has been found of feathered birds flying at that time but some creatures were "*bird-like*" having bodies like birds, long legs with claws and long necks topped with heads shaped like birds. In Australia, the emu, and in South Africa, the ostrich, both flightless birds, are similar to those earlier birds.

About 1,000 years ago in New Zealand, long isolated from other lands by tectonic movement, massive flightless birds called moas roamed the two islands but the first inhabitants, the

Morioris, eventually hunted them to extinction and today the only proof of their existence is found in camp sites and middens.

My neat little explanation of the evolution of birds received a jolt with the announcement by a friend of mine, another diviner, that he had found evidence of the existence of a pre-historic flying bird with a wing-span of about 25 metres on his property in the Dandenong Ranges east of Melbourne. At this stage he has asked to remain anonymous because to reveal his whereabouts would be to invite a flood of professional and amateur fossil hunters.

Before relating the story of my friend - whom I shall call Sam - I ask readers to study the photograph opposite. The lines were marked on the ground with lime after am had traced them with a pendulum. The photograph is of a nest containing several eggs of a pterodactyl which, from other evidence am found, seemed to have a wing-span of roughly 25 metres, about the size of a modern jet air line. If what am found is true and not an hallucination, then not only has world fossil history been rewritten but also the ancient history of Australia.

Forever the sceptic, when I heard Sam's claims I had to reject them as unsubstantiated, a negative attitude which I am sure Sam didn't appreciate. But as we had been close friends for several years and had worked together on many divining projects the least I could do was to listen to his story.

My cautionary attitude stemmed from my having known of a case where a person with an IQ of 135 and holding tertiary qualifications turned to divining and became so obsessed she became schizophrenic, the first signs of which were extravagant imagining.

This is what Sam told me:

> "*My property is on a slight ridge where there are some granite-like boulders. I was intending to build a new*

house and decided to check the area for floating boulders which could interfere with the footings. I found the top of a boulder hidden in the grass so I cleared the area to check its size. Also I wanted to ascertain if there were any other boulders floating in the sub-soil beneath. Soon the pendulum began describing some shapes I'd never come across before in water-divining so I thought I'd better mark them on the ground to get a better idea of what was there. When I had completed the lines I found to my amazement they formed the shape of a gigantic nautilus shell, which I later found existed in the Permian era about 280 million years ago.

After this find I began a systematic survey of the entire property of about five hectares and eventually found the outlines of a whole range of ancient creatures of the Cenozoic era about 65 million years ago, and others of the preceding Cretaceous era, some 70 million years earlier. Three of the outlines were quite remarkable - a small rhinoceros-type animal, a fish and a huge tortoise which seemed to be of the Jurassic period about 200 million years ago. With little knowledge of fossils, the only way I recognised the shapes on the ground was by studying reference books.

Because the lime-covered lines tallied so remarkably with known fossils it seemed to me that some credence had to be given to them. Of course the question arose whether I was reconstructing psychically the outlines of fossils found in other parts of the world, but this would pre-empt knowledge of their shapes which I did not have at that time. Later I read about the doyen of Canadian archaeology, Professor Norman Emerson, locating valuable archeological sites with the aid of the clairvoyant, George McMullen, and I wondered if I too had reacted like McMullen.

Then came a most startling development in my fossil search. One day the pendulum indicated a certain place as the site of a fossil but there was nothing on the surface of the ground. I dug down and found nothing but on leaving. I picked up a tiny pebble which I took back to my study and placed on my desk.

I tried to identify it using a small pendulum but strange-shaped lines which had no meaning seemed to radiate from the pebble. In an effort to see what the shapes of these lines represented I placed the pebble in the centre of a large piece of paper and commenced to draw in the lines indicated by the pendulum. The shape which emerged was like a delicately formed prehistoric quadruped (opposite). The piece of paper proved to be too small to get all the creature in and I had to add other sheets to accommodate the entire drawing.

My being able to draw this creature from a tiny pebble was an exciting break-through for I now realised a diviner could reconstruct the complete shape of an object from only a small portion it. I proved this by breaking a small piece of stone from a rock which I had enlarged into a drawing of a creature and from the fragment was able to replicate the entire drawing.

I must hasten to add that I have little ability in free-hand drawing and the graceful lines of the quadruped seemed as if they had been drawn by another person. It was about this time that I found a round stone shaped like a skull but devoid of a mandible. I laid this on the ground on a similar piece of paper and using the same technique reconstructed the shape of a tall man lying on his back. To check my drawing I turned the stone 90 degrees from its original position and the lines of the body coincided with those in the first drawing. Later I found other stones which gave the outlines of women and children."

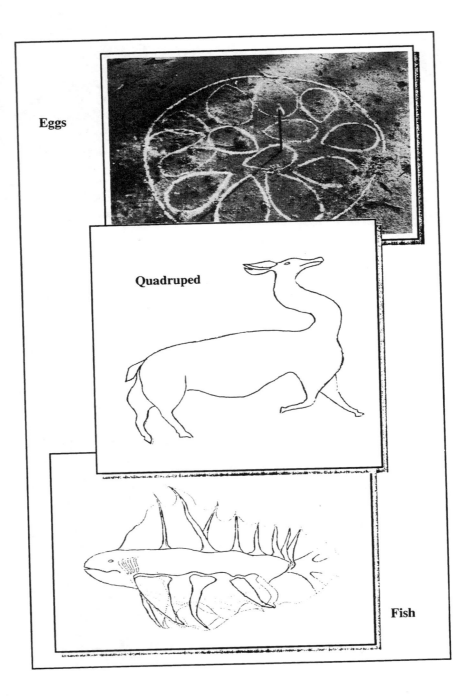

Eggs

Quadruped

Fish

When Sam told me of his finding evidence, which seemed to show the existence of a pre-historical human on his property, I could not accept it. The claim was so way out that I was sure his imagination had run amok, so I asked am to send me a map of his property, which I knew well, and I would try to confirm findings by remote divining.

When the map arrived I began examining it with minute sweeps of the pendulum - the standard remote divining technique. Suddenly the pendulum began to move sideways and I realised something was there. I marked off the area and reproduced it in a much larger scale, and on checking this I soon had drawn in the outline of what appeared to be a small building. Nothing else seemed to be near it so I plotted the exact position of the outline using a corner of Sam's house as a datum to facilitate an on-site check.

When I next visited Sam I went to the corner of his house and with the aid of a tape and a compass located the exact point where my remote survey had shown the building outline. Putting in a marker I commenced to go over the area with an L-wire which immediately turned in the direction of one of the walls. Within 10 minutes I had completed the outline on the ground and it matched perfectly with that on my map.

As I had built a mud-brick cottage I was able to say with certainty that the lines were those of an earth-walled building. The irregularly of the lines indicated its builders had only a primitive knowledge of geometry and building construction. Over the next few months I watched Sam survey a lot of the land around his property and he found many other indications of the existence of other fossils, including signs of human habitation.

Perhaps because of my prejudice I could not get the same pendulum reactions as Sam did, but nevertheless there appeared to be mounting evidence to back his findings. One small stone which he extended into lines on paper revealed the shape of a young man. When I studied this it's similarity to something I'd seen somewhere teased my memory. On returning home I went through all my books on ancient history, then went to the reference section of the Bendigo Public Library where eventually the name Pompeii popped up. Then I remembered. Sam's drawing resembled the shape of one of the bodies which had been located during the excavation of the city which had been obliterated by volcanic ash during the 79AD eruption of nearby Vesuvius.

These bodies were in the position in which they fell after asphyxiation by the sulphurous gases from the eruption and the agonised expressions on their faces and twisted limbs were similar to those of am's young man. Subsequently I questioned am closely on his knowledge of Pompeii. Not only had he never been to the city but had not seen pictures of the mouldings of the bodies in its museum of relics. One of Sam's greatest finds was a small piece of rock the shape of a finger which a radiographer in Melbourne x-rayed and said he was convinced it was part of a human finger.

With my scepticism waning under the impact of all this evidence I made a particular study of the outline of the nest of pterodactyl eggs. The way the way the eggs overlapped in the nest was perplexing and am could not explain it. So I got half a dozen eggs out of the fridge and put them in a small round basket. They overlapped when the eggs were placed at different levels, and when viewed from above their outlines were identical with those of Sam's pterodactyl eggs.

I have no doubt that Sam is what is known as a "sensitive" and I hope that eventually circumstances will prevail when he will be able to reveal the full extent of his findings without either being subjected to personal ridicule or jeopardising the privacy of home and property. Since completing this work on fossils Sam has moved into the field of geological exploration and some of his findings are as original and thought-provoking as his work on the fossils.

Atlantis - fact or fancy ?

The Pillars of Hercules stand at the western end of the Mediterranean Sea, geographically identified today as Punta Tarifa on the Spanish side and Punta Almina on the Tangier side. Between them lies the Strait of Gibraltar, probably one of two most famous maritime passageways in the world, the other being the Bosphorus.

The name the Pillars of Hercules was common in the time of the Greek philosopher, Plato, whose Academy founded in 387 BC, was based on the Socratic method of using debate to reveal inconsistencies in logic. In Plato's record of one such debate, between Timaeus and Critias, before Socrates, he reports Critias' account of the legend of Atlantis.

Critias relied on a story attributed to Solon, an Athenian statesman who had lived some 200 years before. Solon had heard about the existence of Atlantis and its subsequent destruction by a cataclysmic geological upheaval about 10,000 BC on a visit to Egypt. Solon said an elderly priest told him:

> "*There were earthquakes and floods of extraordinary violence, and in a single dreadful day and night all your fighting men (Athenians) were swallowed up by the earth, and the island of Atlantis was similarly swallowed up by the sea and vanished; this is why the sea in that area is to this day impassable to navigation, which is hindered by mud just below the surface, the remains of the sunken island.*"

One of Plato's disciples, Krantor, claimed to have seen an Egyptian inscription at Sais which was said to have been a record of the history of Atlantis. The Egyptian origin of the Atlantis story ties in with the writings of the famous 17th-century philosopher, Athanasius Kircher, who was one of the first linguists to translate early Egyptian writing.

Kircher, a brilliant mathematician and historian, was said to have had an "insatiable curiosity about ancient cultures." Among the papers found after his death in Rome in 1680 was a map of Atlantis (see opposite). In the third century AD the famous Roman historian, Marcellinus, described the "swallowing up of a large island" in the Atlantic. Other historians attributed the advanced astronomical abilities of the ancient Mexicans to Atlantean scientists.

The existence of Atlantis remained largely anecdotal until 1890 when the Atlantic cable was being laid. When it broke about 500 miles north of the Azores, a mechanical grab trying to retrieve one end, brought up some rocks later identified by geologists as lava which had solidified in air. Then in 1956 Dr Rene Malaise, of the Riks Museum, Stockholm, announced that he and his colleague Dr P. W. Kolbe, had found that earth cores taken from under the sea near the Azores contained material which could have existed only in freshwater lakes and rivers. They dated the material at about 12,000 years old - about the era described by Plato in Timaeus and Critias.

After World War 2, Major General Jim Scott Elliott, who had won international recognition for his archeological discoveries by means of divining, investigated the legend of Atlantis, and using the remote map divining technique with a pendulum, made the map (see page 117).

My interest in Atlantis began inconsequently through having to feed a couple of parakeets owned by Dr Michael Homewood. A friend and I looked after his modest fibro-cement home while he and his family holidayed in Fiji. Before leaving, the doctor introduced us to his feathered pets which bore the unlikely names of Timaeus and Critias.

My daily duties consisted of giving them bird seed and water and placing newspaper in the bottom of their cage to collect their droppings. Why the doctor had named the birds Timaeus and Critias is beyond comprehension as their screeching was the direct opposite to a Socratean interlocution, and their indiscriminate contributions to the letter columns of The Age were a loosely constructed premise to any argument.

The birds and I developed a mutual antipathy, which peaked when I renamed them "*Ugly*" and "*Orrible*." I can imagine the bewilderment of the good doctor when he returned from Fiji to find that his parakeets regarded him with wide-eyed paranoia.

The words Timaeus and Critias, thus being etched on my mind, found me reaching for the book when I stumbled across it in the local library. Being a diviner with a keen interest in unsolved mysteries, I began wondering, as did Scott Elliott, if indeed Atlantis had ever existed and whether it were possible to locate its original whereabouts by means of long-range map prospecting. With a tracing from the *Macquarie World Atlas* I made a cursory prospection and found there seemed to be something resembling an island to the west of the coasts of Spain and Africa. I filed away the map I had made and then forgot about it.

It was not until some two years later when I was working with the clairvoyant Jill Foster the subject of the lost continent of Atlantis came up and we decided to see what a dual effort of a diviner and a clairvoyant would achieve. Incidentally we seemed ideally suited for such an experiment as Jill said she had only heard of Atlantis but had no idea where it was thought to have been.

To ensure that she was not prompted by my original map of the island I covered an extensive area of the Atlantic Ocean to the west of Spain and North Africa with opaque white paper and asked her if she would move her hand across the area to ascertain if she reacted in any way.

With eyes closed, Jill opened her right hand and with the palm down began moving it from the coast of North American towards Europe. When her hand seemed to be just over half way across she stopped. *"There's something here,"* she exclaimed, adding, *"This is wonderful. It feels like home."*

Moving her hand around in small circles, she kept repeating, *"This is a good feeling."* A few seconds later her hand stopped still. Jill's expression changed to one of pain and she cried out: *"Oh, this is awful. All I see is red. Everything is red. An explosion. A terrible explosion. We must get away. Escape!"*

Then she jerked away her hand and cried out: *"I've got to stop. This feels too terrible."* A few seconds later Jill opened her eyes and I could see she was almost crying. As I pulled away the paper away, she added almost reflectively: *"What a terrible waste, So many people, Gone."*

Where the centre of her palm had been was the island I had picked out with my pendulum as the island of Atlantis. (My drawing is on the next page.)

Both Jill and I realise that historically our experiment is scientifically unsupportable, just another straw in the Atlantis wind, but no-one who had been present would have doubted the sincerity of her emotional reaction to the experience of our experiment.

Had she really gone back in time to when she lived on Atlantis some 12,000 years ago, or was it all a figment of her imagination stimulated by a mental telepathic import from myself? Who knows. All I can say is that I am left with an intuitive certainty that the island of Atlantis indeed did exist to the west of the Pillars of Hercules, as Plato stated, and that it was destroyed in a violent volcanic eruption. The one real aspect of Jill's and my experiment was her personal distress which can never be explained away as fiction.

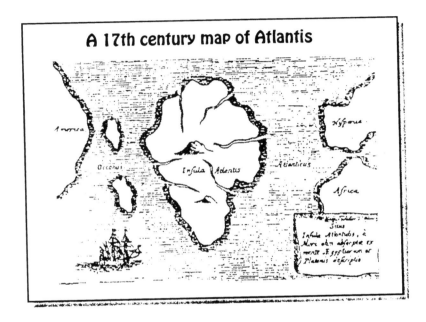

A 17th century map of Atlantis

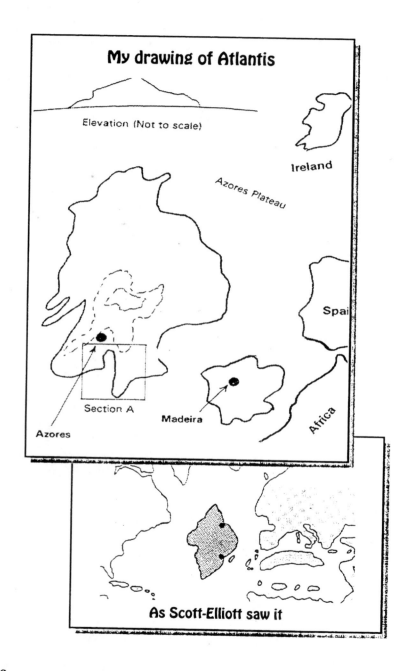

My drawing of Atlantis

Elevation (Not to scale)

Ireland

Azores Plateau

Spai

Section A

Madeira

Azores

Africa

As Scott-Elliott saw it

Lost and found

The tiny shire of Bet Bet in Central Victoria, within whose boundaries my mudbrick cottage was situated, was but a tiny mouse compared with the lion of a rural city but although small its sense of civic pride was large.

Over the years its shire councillors, eight in number, made many momentous decisions affecting the life and times of its citizens but few affected Newbridge which slumbered on beside the glutinous waters of the Loddon River. Alas, with amalgamation to improve beauracratic efficiency, Bet Bet has now been absorbed into the greater Shire of Korong and its autonomy has vanished under the iron heel of progress.

One of its momentous decisions was to add to the beauty of the township of Newbridge (158 souls, plus domestic animals and stock). A grass verge about 50 metres long was to be rotary-hoed and some trees planted to replace those which had died through lack of water. This time there would be no mistake; new trees would edge the road through Newbridge and be watered regularly to make the township an inspiring gateway to the flood of tourists expected from the east.

A few years ago it was the fashion to add an appellation to the name of every rural city and town to attract the interest of tourists, whose spending sprees were seen as a potential source of wealth. Poetical allusions, alliterations and rhymes poured forth from the city fathers and mothers describing these rural centres and the results of their literary efforts are now to be seen all over Australia.

This was a bit like the bumper sticker fad which came and went. They began with descriptions of the states themselves. There is the "*The Sunshine State*," "*The Premier State*," and so on. Victoria was called "*The Garden State*" but at one time it was better known as "*The Bankrupt State*," and the "*State of Despair*."

However, things are better now there's been a change of Government and a few of its assets have been sold. Originally Melbourne was bought from the Aborigines for a handful of beads and trinkets but market indicators show it should be worth a little more now.

Bet Bet chose for the central town, Dunolly, the name "*The Centre of the Golden Grain*," it being both a gold mining and wheat-growing area. When it came to Newbridge, the councillors were stumped until one of them recalled its annual fishing competition in which competitors finished up at the "*local*" where they endeavoured to out-do the fish. And so Newbridge became: "*The Fishermen's Haven*." Exactly what part of the town that refers does not test one's acumen.

One exceedingly hot day when the temperature was hovering in the sweltering 40's, I was returning home after an early shift at the Bendigo Advertiser and idly trying to decide whether to drop into the "*local*" for a frosty pot of Fosters or return home and cut some fence posts.

Parking under a huge peppercorn tree in the centre of the road adjoining the pub, I noticed a worthy citizen digging frantically in the grass verge outside his home. This was such an intriguing spectacle in heat that I ventured across the road and raised a speculative eyebrow. Ask a silly question and one gets a silly answer, for the worthy one replied thus: "*What the bloody hell do you think I'm doing? Digging for, gold?*"

Then in a few short sentences he gave an off-the-record opinion of the city fathers, their parentage or lack of it and an assessment of their individual and collective IQ's, which didn't require taking off one's shoes to add up.

"The bloody idiots rotary-hoed the verge and cut through my pipe running down to the river pump and now I can't find it," Quoth the digger, who had made the newly turned earth look like a high-rise rabbit warren.

Ever the good samaritan I whisked home, returned with a bent coat-hanger and within a couple of minutes had not only located the pipe but pegged the exact section which had been chewed into black specs. The miraculous skills of *"Mud-brick Dick,"* were chorused up and down the public bar and much free thirst-quenching ale came my way. The exercise had its interesting side as I had never divined for plastic before and had found this could be located with an L-wire as easily as finding an underground stream.

At one stage in my working life I had had a break from journalism by working as an assistant painter in an oil refinery at Newport, a West Melbourne suburb. The refinery, the smallest in Australia, nestled against the flank of the huge Shell distribution installation, and made a living by blending a few lubricating cocktails from base stock bought from its neighbour.

On joining the refinery I asked where I could find the painter whom I was to assist and was told: *"You're it."* In the following five years I painted everything from tanks to buildings, fences, an old house, in fact everything that was static. Several times I painted myself, especially on one occasion when I was at the top of a 30-ft ladder which slipped down the side of a building I was painting.

My most memorable day in this job was when I upset a bucket of turpentine over my crotch, the heat of which nearly set both me and the refinery ablaze.

A newly appointed managing director instigated a policy of property beautification, part of which required me to spray-paint a 20-ft high wire fence. I tested the way the wind was blowing and commenced spraying it a beautiful silver when the wind swung viciously to the south and I became indistinguishable from the fence. At this moment the MD drove up in his silver Mercedes and on alighting saw his silver painter backgrounded by the silver fence. With an executive's decision-making he said; *Before you clean up you'd better turn over all the bits of gravel which are silver.*

The company's history was peppered with similar momentous decisions, like one by the founder who on a visit to New York saw automatic shoe-shine machines, which he imported in great numbers.

The only problem was that they were powered by direct current and by the time they were unshipped in Melbourne the city had swung over to alternating current and there were no AC motors of the right size available. The crates of shoe-shine machines were dumped in an old watchman's house in the refinery grounds and to mention their existence was to court immediate sacking.

Roaming around the refinery's extensive grounds the MD noticed that the driveways were uneven so he ordered them to be levelled. The first we knew of this second managerial decree was when a huge road-grader commenced scraping away everything in sight.

So thorough was the job that when it was finished every marker placed in the ground to indicate the whereabouts of underground pipes was gone.

In the following months, the repair of each pipeline or joint required much digging. One afternoon when there was no more gravel to be turned over I made an L-wire and located and marked every underground oil, water and chemical pipe and also electric and telephone wires and entered them on the drawing with a colour code to identify each. Identification was made by counting the time a pendulum oscillated over each, and matching the counts originated by the Abbe Mermet. Here is a list of his counts:

Identification counts

Item	Count	Item	Count
Sex, male	12	Sex, female	6
Human body	19	Brain	20
Heart	12	Lung	10
Stomach	7	water	7
Iron, steel	4	Limestone	4.4
Aluminium	5	Nickel	5
Cavities	6	Silver	6
Copper, bronze	7	Tin	7
Glass	9	Sodium chloride	12
Potassium	13	Chromium	14
Petroleum gas	14	Mercury	15
Phosphates	17	Zinc	17
Sulphur	18	Lead	21
Radioactive bodies	22	Crude petroleum	22
Carbon, graphite, coal, diamond	30		

It will be noticed that some of the counts are identical. This is because the intuitive mind modulates incoming signals to a hertz range which can be interpreted by the conscious mind.

Much of my experience in using divining to find lost articles occurred at Newbridge and in many experiments I was assisted by my neighbour, George Davies. But now George, who became one of the closest friends I've ever had, is dead. I did not learn this for some months after I had left the town as I'm not given to read the deceased columns in newspapers. Immediately I drove out to see his widow, Mavis, and on the way I saw the sign "*Cemetery*," so I stopped.

There was no headstone reading George Clifford Davies and I wondered if I was in the right place. It was winter and raining and I was getting saturated. Then I saw the pile of glutenous, yellow clay and immediately I knew he lay beneath it. It was the cold anonymity of this little patch of Newbridge which tore at the heart.

George had been one of those rare gregarious characters whose moral strength, kindness and tolerance had been a model for the 160 people in the town for nearly 60 years. But now George, jocularly known as "*The Mayor of Newbridge*," was gone. Although my face was wet I couldn't help smiling, for somehow George seemed to be present. I could feel the aura of his personality around me and I couldn't help speaking to him: "*George, it must be cold down there.*" I can still hear his reply: "*Trust me to forget my coat.*"

George had helped me in many experiments in divining, especially in developing a technique for finding lost articles. But first a little about this small man who had lived his life steadfastly and with a quiet sense of humour which never seemed to desert him.

He was born on a smallholding in the district at some 18 years before Australia was involved in the Second World War. He joined the army and through being a footballer and not adverse to physical contact he went into a commando unit.
When the war ended he was a paratrooper trained to operate behind enemy lines. After demobilisation he began growing tomatoes and eventually through hard work and a native shrewdness became one of the biggest and most successful growers in the district.

I met him when I drifted south from Mildura in the north of the State, where I'd gone after the break-up of my marriage. I asked him if there were any blocks of land for sale and he offered me a small one adjoining his property. It was the site of a huge brick factory but now covered with boxthorn bushes, heaps of broken bricks and old car bodies.

He said I could have it at half the going rate for land in Newbridge so I bought it. The construction of a small mud-brick cottage, which earned me the name of *"Mudbrick Dick,"* would not have occurred without George's support, encouragement and friendship. To give you an idea of how rough that block was I had 140 tonnes of rubble removed before I could get my car and caravan onto it.

George allowed me to buy water which he pumped from the nearby Loddon River and supplied me with electric power until I settled in. Because our lands adjoined we used to cut across each other's blocks and many were the times we stopped and yarned. Typical of George's humour was a brawl which occurred between two women in his packing shed.

I was listening in amazement to the screaming, yelling and crashes from the shed when I saw a door open and amid a fusillade of flying tomatoes George emerged and slouched towards me. Stopping for his usual *"G'day,"* he left it to me to raise an eyebrow towards the mounting cacophony in the packing shed.

He looked at me with a wry twinkle in his eyes and without letting his face slip he said: " *Seems the girls don't agree about something.*" With that he went on his way, not returning until war had ended either through the combatants' exhaustion or their supplies of tomatoes had dried up.

On another occasion I was driving him into Bendigo some 35 kilometres distant when he pointed to a tiny, isolated house in the distance standing near an old gnarled peppercorn tree. "*I started as a farmhand there when was 14,*" he said, adding, "*Of course, it was only the night life which kept me there.*"

One day George came over to me in quite a fluster. His pump on the river Loddon had broken down and he needed his shifting spanner but couldn't find it.

"*Can I borrow yours, Dick*," he said. "*Of course*," I replied but suddenly I remembered I had loaned mine to a mate who was trying to fix his circular saw in the bush.

George said he had been working on an automatic seeder in one of his paddocks but on returning home found he'd left the shifter somewhere in the grass. He'd searched the area without success. "*How about trying with your divining wire?*" he asked.

We walked to where George had been working and found the grass was about 30 cm high, enough to hide even a brick from sight. I held the L-wire in front of me and concentrated on finding his shifter. Despite the strong wind the wire began to move against the wind and pointed.

I asked George to stand where I had been while I moved about five metres away. Again the wire pointed but this time slightly back towards George giving an intersection point. As I reached this point I actually stood on the shifter.

Not long after, a friend, Margaret Loughnan, asked me to help her check a block of land she was considering buying near Chewton, south of Bendigo. We were treading through the dead grass when we saw a patch of lush green grass in the centre of the block.

There had to be a source of water for this grass and I asked Margaret if she had any wire in the car. She produced a coathanger from which I made an L-wire and in no time I was tracing an underground stream. I followed it for some 500 metres and until it ended at a rocky sump at the back of a group of dog kennels.

126

When the kennels were washed out, the urine and faeces flowed into a sump which leached under the adjoining road to the block Margaret was thinking of buying. Oddly she did not enthuse over having this free source of fertiliser.

When we returned to the car Margaret said in a small voice: "*I think I've lost the car key.*"

We searched everywhere even walking back to the kennels but there was no sign of them. As I was holding the divining wire in my hand I thought I would try to see if I could locate the missing keys with it. Immediately I held out the wire it swung to the left and where it pointed I found the keys. Even today I'm not sure if Margaret lost the keys or was testing my divining ability but it doesn't matter because I didn't know where the keys were and I found them with the L-wire.

Back at Newbridge I began a series of experiments getting people to hide articles of different materials for me to locate with L-wire and pendulum and recorded the results. At first my success rate was poor but, as with all aspects of divining, it improved greatly with practice.

On one occasion my sister Pat and her husband Bob called and I told them what I was doing. This was greeted with open derision and Bob immediately asked me to go inside my cottage while he hid something. I complied and on being told to emerge I picked up the L-wire and it pointed exactly to where he had hidden his car keys under a pile of crushed bluestone.

They tested me several times then hurriedly dropped the subject of divining and I saw them look at each other with a meaningful shake of the head. Obviously I was heading for the nut house. Instead of parking their caravan on my property they took it across the river to the football ground!

Over the years I have learned much about searching for lost articles and not a few times have been caught by not being thorough in my divining. One particular case occurred in a Warrnambool caravan park only a couple of years ago. I had been working on the car but when I came to start it the keys were nowhere to be found. I obtained a piece of wire and began a systematic search.

Everywhere I went the L-wire pointed to the pillar on the left side of the car but although I shifted everything, seat included, I could not find the keys. There was nothing for it but to buy another set so I drove some 10 kilometres into the town, parked outside a locksmith and gave him my spare set to copy.

When I was taking the new set of keys out to the car I happened to glance upwards and there were my missing keys sitting in the roof gutter immediately above the left-hand pillar. They had been there all the time and had not moved, even during the journey into town. The moral is: when looking for something with either a pendulum or L-wire you must look both upwards and downwards in the direction to which a divining instrument seem to be pointing.

One of the problems with finding lost articles is that if the diviner personally owns them then he or she will be emotionally upset by the loss and so the search will begin with the diviner being emotionally upset, if only slightly. This is enough to affect any result. Often too a diviner is unsure which way a wire or pendulum points. For example, an L-wire points a different way in each hand. Only the cultivation of a detached attitude and experience with divining wires will overcome these problems.

Love
"There's many a slip"

"Let's fall in love. Why don't we fall in love?" But hang on. What would Granny say about this? Being a grandpa I can tell you. She would put down her knitting and looking wisely over her glasses, and give forth with a bit of knife-under-the-bed wisdom, such as: *"There's many a slip 'tween cup and lip."* Likewise, *" Many a mickle makes a muckle."* Also, *"A stitch in time saves nine."*

Back to your knitting, Granny. But to be fair, she might have something, especially if you look at the current marriage break-up statistics. About 50 per cent of first marriages fail, and the figure for second marriages is about 75 per cent.

Where, oh, where do we go wrong? Whom can we blame?. When it comes to apportioning blame, then, if we are honest, the ball lies fairly and squarely in our court - the people who are stuffing up everything. Not necessarily our partners, no, it's us - you and me. But the big, big problem is how can we make decisions in the marriage market so that we don't merely become another failure statistic?

But first it must be asked: is it possible for two people who are emotionally attracted to each to decide whether or not they have a future together?

Personally, I think the chances of winning Tattslotto or winning Russian Roulette, played with a machine pistol, are better. The problem is that if there is any emotional interest in a result whatsoever then the answer must be distorted accordingly. However if it is simply the case of a diviner deciding if he or she could be compatible with a stranger, then the chances of a correct answer are good. Of course if the diviner begins his or her assessment having already become prejudiced because of another person's physical characteristics then emotions are involved with the inevitable result. So it is apparent that using a pendulum to help choose a partner is fraught with difficulties. A bit like trying to walk on pigeon's eggs without crunching them. However with some understanding as to why people are attracted to each other the chances of a successful pendular selection improve.

Another diviner and I conducted a series of joint and independent experiments in pendular assessment of attraction and compatibility between ourselves and other people and the result were better than average. But when we came to assessing relationships between other people we had to acknowledge that any judgment we made would have to be subjective and so unacceptably biased.

One of the most illuminating studies ever made was by a group of American family psychologists who produced what they called the Family Systems Exercise. The British family therapist, Robin Skynner, who with entertainer, John Cleese, of Fawlty Towers fame, wrote "*Families and How to Survive Them,*" related how it works.

A group of 20 men and 20 women were asked to circulate around a room and without speaking choose someone who made them think of a person in their own family or someone who filled a missing space in their family.

Next they had to go to the person they had chosen and discuss with them why they had made the choice and learn something about each other and their backgrounds. Each of them found they had chosen someone who had a remarkably similar background.

The next step involved each couple choosing another couple in the same manner, and then the foursomes had to sit together and hold a similar discussion. The same thing was found - each foursome selected each other because of the background similarities. Skynner said that in the experiment in which he took part four people were left over.

When these explained why they had not chosen anyone it was revealed that each was a loner and as such had similar family backgrounds including divorced and/or deserted parents.

What actually happened in this exercise is that light wave energy was reflected from the facial expressions, body postures and movements of each of these people into the retinas of the others. From there the energy was conveyed via optic nerves to their brains where it was intuitively analysed and interpreted. This led to conscious reactions of either affinity or rejection.

In addition to this visual data was the invisible and over ridingly powerful projections from people's personalities. It is ironical to think that all this subtle energy interaction resulted eventually in verbal read-outs, such as: " *Wow. What a hunk.*""*She's cool.*" Or perhaps: " *Yuk.*"

Those who want to play the dangerous game of judging others or even themselves should bear in mind the old proverb: "*Judge not, or ye will not be judged*" - a warning wrapped in subtlety. In our experiments we used a simple system of percentage assessments, a technique which has many applications.

Oscar Wilde, who these days would have been queen of Sydney's Gay Mardi Gras, came up with an epigram which can be applied in compatibility judgments. "*It is only shallow people who do not judge by appearances.*"

On one occasion my own appearance left a lot to be desired. A spotty 17-year-old, I went to a local dance in Murrumbeena, a southern suburb of Melbourne, and although rather short I wound up with a dream in white chiffon who must have been about 1.80m high.

After finding conversing with her navel rather one-sided I thought I would impress her with my *"Fred Astaire"* spin turn but something went wrong and I fell against a wall, hit the bevel of a picture which crashed over my head. The look Ginger Rogers gave me from her prone position on the dance floor with her head half under a bench suggested my appearance at the dance had a lot to be desired.

From my studies I have concluded that divining has only a very limited use in assessing human relationships. I use a pendulum merely to try to establish the percentage potential of people remaining together in a contented and rewarding relationship. The method is detailed opposite.

However I would stress that because the diviner is dealing with human emotions he or she must be completely objective otherwise results are certain to be misleading and could cause great unhappiness. This is one case where a diviner should never offer an opinion unless asked, and then the possibility of error must be fully explained to the person asking the question.

Percentage assessments

Every diviner should practice this system of assessing percentages as it can be applied to many different investigations. Here is how it is done:

People use the numbers 0-100 in many different ways. Here are just a few: time, temperatures, distances and all manner of statistics. All we do is program our minds as to what we want the 0-100 to represent. It's a bit like the way we pick up a piece of paper with a few squiggles on it and say to ourselves: " This is a map." In divining it's handy to use 0-100 millimetres on an ordinary rule to represent percentages. All the diviner does it hold the pendulum over the 0 until it oscillates then move it along until a certain percentage is indicated, say 65% as in example below. Now begin again saying that zero equals 60 degrees and the 0-10 equals a total of 10 degrees. You can keep on going until you reach whatever degree of exactitude you require.

Move pendulum along until it
begins to swing sideways

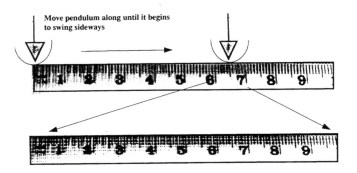

This numerical-pendular system can be used for many purposes in a variety of applications

All that glisters is not gold

The search for gold has ensnared the hopes of man since the earliest of civilisations. Diviners have not been immune from the desire to obtain this *"free"* source of wealth, least of all myself.

I live in what is called the *"Golden Triangle"* of Northern Victoria which was one of the most prolific producers of gold in the late 19th and early 20th centuries. However, with inadequate machinery the inrush of groundwater eventually beat the miners and before the Second World War even the biggest mines were forced to close.

A few mining companies persisted with alluvial production but it was nothing like the heyday when one small blacksmiths shop in Iron Bark, to the west of Bendigo, used to sharpen more than 200 compressed-air tools a day. Two old-timers still work at their forge but it is now used for sharpening picks, and crowbars and casting fire grates.

One particular company, Bendigo Mining NL, had a few leases when I settled in the area in 1983. Its biggest was at Mt Moliagul, some 100 kilometres to the west near where the famous *"Welcome Stranger"* nugget - a 2,300 ounce monster - was found. This was so big it had to be cut up for transport to Melbourne. The anvil is now a monument in the nearby town of Dunolly.

I had read of the exploits of the French Catholic priest, the Abbe Mermet, in gold detection by divining and I thought I would try out my water divining skills to find a few ounces or perhaps another monster nugget!

After several abortive attempts I had several talks with the principals of Bendigo Mining and they agreed to my experimenting by trying to peg the gold reefs on their Moliagul lease. The lease lies abreast of indicators - blue slate veins - which originate at the famous Ballarat Goldfields.

I had no knowledge as to whether I was correctly pegging the reefs until I came on a huge pit being dug by the company to *"paddock"* the lease. Paddocking is the removal of all top and subsoil for mechanical centrifuge gold extraction. One of my top reefs cut across this pit at the bottom of which I could see where an excavator had broken the surrounding matrix.

My divining efforts were closely watched by a very sceptical supervisor who had reluctantly lent me some white-topped pegs for marking the reefs when and if I found them. After I had pegged four reefs the supervisor came over to me and told me the story of the original prospector, a 70-year-old man, who had found an extraordinarily rich pocket of gold nuggets near the northern end of the lease.

I traversed a wide area and finally came on what appeared to be a small reef running parallel into the others in a north-westerly direction as most of the reefs in the Northern Victoria do. I pegged this reef and told the supervisor who then took me to a spot 200 metres away. *"I know where the reef indicator is. Let me see if you can find it,"* he said.

Whenever a diviner is put to the test by a sceptic he or she has a sinking feeling. All diviners know that they can fail and also that during the course of a day a wire or pendulum will lie dead in their hands as if the energy has gone out of their arms. Clearly to the supervisor this was a crucial test. Finding reefs, only one of which was evident, could have been luck but here was something he knew about. With hands on hips he watched me hold out my L-wire and commence surveying the area.

I don't know why it is but I've always felt slightly surprised when I locate a target, as if I was sceptically watching another diviner at work as I was being watched at that moment. I was feeling like this when I experienced a sudden tingling sensation in my arm and the wire kicked sideways. I marked where the wire indicated with some stones and pieces of bark then traced a line along the ground, marking it with the end of a branch. To my gratification the line ran north-west to south-east, following the direction of the other reefs in the lease.

My work seemed to relax the supervisor who, dropping down on his haunches and pulling out a cigarette, told me the story of the old-timer. He said the old man had to leave his reef and go into hospital and while he was there he confided to a friend that the mine was a bonanza.

However while he was in hospital a torrential rainstorm flooded the entire lease, several feet deep in some places, and turned a nearby stream into a raging torrent. When the water subsided there was no sign of where the little mine had been. Everything had been washed away and the mine filled in.

The old man was broken hearted and although he made several attempts to find it, eventually age and ill health forced him to give up. The supervisor and I dug down where I had pegged the indicators and found one of the widest grey-blue slate lines I'd ever seen. Mostly these indicators are mere thin lines of slate increasing sometimes to three or four centimetres in width but this was about 15 centimetres wide and broke up in big chunks.

While I gained no reward in pegging the company's reefs on the lease the exercise provided invaluable experience and led to the discovery of a peculiar phenomenon about gold reefs which generally consist of the metal embedded in a matrix of quartz.

136

When tracing the course of a subterranean reef the divining wires will indicate a break in the matrix which is sometimes quite wide.

I did not understand what this meant until I went to the place nearby where the *"Welcome Stranger"* nugget was found. I began divining in circles in an attempt to locate the mother-reef from which it had originated. Eventually I found a significant reef some 50 metres to the east and to my surprise it had a break in it about three metres wide.

In the course of the next three years I went to many places where gold nuggets had been found and in nearly every case there was a reef to the east with a break in it. The question then arose as to why should large and small masses of gold break away from a reef and always move upwards? It seems to me that significant accumulations of gold in the quartz matrix creates a weakness which is the first place in the reef to shatter when an earth tremor or quake occurs.

It seems logical that the constant turning of the earth towards the east causes the heavy gold mass to increasingly lag behind the reef proper until eventually the two are separated by a significant distance - as in the case of the *"Welcome Stranger"* and its mother reef.

From this point onwards I was *"hooked"* on gold prospecting believing it was only a matter of time before my L-wire would lead me to a fortune. It was about that time I began to work with another enthusiastic diviner and over the next 18 months we covered nearly every known gold field in the Golden Triangle north-west of Bendigo both with no success at all.

We were encouraged in our determination to solve the problem of divining for gold by the manager of Bendigo Mining who lent me gold nuggets of specific weights over weekends so that we could further our experiments. Our first stumbling block was what the good Abbe called gold's *"magnetic images."* He had found that gold nuggets and articles buried in the ground gave misleading indications of their position.

While the Abbe maintained this confusion was caused by magnetic influences in the atmosphere which increased markedly when sun spots occurred, we believed that it was the spread of isotopic radiation.

We knew that gold was one of the elements which released isotopic radiation which could be identified by a scintillation counter and believed that such radiations from the atoms of gold lumped together as nuggets would give similar read outs to those spread homogeneously through auriferous ground.

Any diviner confronted with a barrage of these radiations would find identifying their exact source almost an impossibility. This was borne out by the fact that we could locate gold nuggets and gold-plated articles, like cufflinks, resting on top of the ground with comparative ease.

To test our theory we placed nuggets in holes and the moment we covered them up our divining wires became disorientated. This was very frustrating especially to my mate, who, with indefatigable energy, dug countless holes in the concrete-hard ground following gold radiations only to find they appeared to shift outside the hole or sometimes seemingly disappear, leaving him with only blistered hands and a raging thirst for all his efforts.

Our experiments in divining for gold led to some amusing incidents. In the area in which we were prospecting there were several abandoned deep shafts and in trying to establish a technique for depthing gold nuggets and reefs these seemed to offer an ideal opportunity, especially as the ground in the general gold-reef area was like concrete and any hole dug by someone else was a not-to-be-missed bonus. But the problem was unless there was gold or a reef in one of the holes we had no target on which to home in on.

Then we had a bright idea, and I was dispatched at once to Bendigo to get the necessary equipment. I first went home and got my fishing rod and then went to a lingerie shop in Bendigo's main street.

A most attractive young woman approached me with a smile which on seeing my dirty bush clothes and old boots seemed to loose some of it's warmth. *"Can I help you, sir,"* she said. *"Yes. I want a pair of panty hose, please." "What size,"* she said. *"It's immaterial,"* I replied.

This seemed to strike at the very heart of her couturial standards for she then gave me a brief but pointed lecture on the construction of panty hose. Having made her point with this despicable male chauvinist pig, the interrogation continued: *"what colour?" "It's immaterial."*

"The colour of panty hose is not immaterial to a woman," she thrust back at me. *"Your wife or girl friend* (and the tone suggested that either case was most unlikely) *will be most annoyed if you take home panty hose which do not match her ensemble."*

By now my patience was beginning to wear a bit thin and I threw a spanner into the verbal battle thus: *"Lady, do you know what I intend to do with the panty hose? I intend to cut them in half and after dropping a nugget into one leg, attach it to a fishing line and drop it down a mine shaft."*

The atmosphere froze. With a distinctly old-fashioned look she hurriedly handed me the panty hose, took the money and fled. Obviously my ability to communicate with the opposite sex matched my skill as a gold diviner.

We dropped stockings containing nuggets down many shafts but the result was always the same - the moment the nugget dropped below earth level, we lost contact with it.

On one occasion a stocking containing nuggets weighing nearly half an ounce and valued at about $A350 got snagged on a rock some 50 metres down the shaft and did we sweat. Eventually it came free and we called it quits for the day.

An interesting aspect of divining for gold is the energy rings around gold and the parallel lines contiguous to gold reefs. Walking away from gold there are 10 distinct kicks of the wire or pendulum with the next one being quite emphatic.

On either side of a gold reef there are 10 parallel lines with the next similarly being a more emphatic line. It seems as if these rings and lines are a signature to gold. This agreed with the findings of the Abbe Mermet who also found that the signature for subterranean fresh water was a system of seven rings and lines.

One major hindrance we had to contend with was that the anticipation of imminent reward hung like a carrot over all our efforts. To be successful in any divining venture a person must be emotionally detached from the result.

If the diviner has even the slightest pecuniary interest in finding anything, especially gold, then he or she unconsciously programs the mind accordingly and tends to get a positive reading in everything he or she does. We were unashamedly interested in finding gold, especially after all the effort we had programmed ourselves to fail. Wisdom in hindsight !

We became very adept at finding gold reefs and one of the techniques used was map divining. We used to obtain survey maps of the gold-bearing region and would mark on the maps the reefs we believed existed and then we would set out in the car to find them.

The problem which had to be overcome was how to measure an exact distance from cross roads. The odometer in the car was useless as it registered in tenths of a kilometre so we obtained the front wheel of a bicycle to which we affixed a revolution counter.

Our technique was for one of us to drive while the other held the wheel in contact with the roadway by keeping the passenger door open. A simple calculation gave the precise distance travelled.

My friend and I tried divining from a moving car. One of us would drive while the other held the divining wire in front of him. We travelled hundreds of kilometres in this way often drawing most curious stares from pedestrians and other road users. One remarkable exploit was when we followed radiations emanating from an area north of the famous gold town of Wedderburn.

We tracked these radiations from four different directions and they all wound up at the same place, the centre of an innocuous looking paddock at Wichetella. With the permission of the farmer we traversed that paddock until we seemed to know every blade of grass, finally pegging what we thought were interesting points.

When we were about to leave we decided to check the land towards the east and sure enough we found strong evidence of a big reef some 500 feet under the ground. Idly we were wandering along the reef line with our wires when my mate called out; *"I've found a break in the reef."*

We marked the break and with a compass we sighted towards the west and sure enough we could see one of our marker flags. We researched our find using surface and map detection techniques and realised what we had found was the re-emergence of the rich *"Black reef"* which was the source of all Wedderburn's gold. However the reef was some 200 metres deep and so precluded further prospecting.

By some quirk of human nature the word *"Gold"* has a strange effect on men and women. The kindly, the genial and the timid immediately metamorphose into scheming, immoral and greedy beings, a Dr Jekyll and Mr Hyde transformation which gives understanding to the motivation of bushrangers and other desperadoes who will even murder to get their hands on the precious metal.

In the course of our experimentation in gold divining I've come across quite a few of these characters and was amazed at the cunning with which they planned and executed their thefts.

It was Shakespeare who had he hapless Prince of Morocco say *"All that glisters is not gold."* One Bendigo man who warranted the Australian Order of Merit for conmanship proved there were two sides to this quip of wisdom. He sold a mine and all its equipment for nearly $750,000 based on the rich gold showing in a quartz vein. How did that glitter get there?

This villain refilled numerous shotgun cartridges with gold dust and fired them at the quartz vein thereby impregnating it with gold until it resembled a richly impregnated matrix. It always seemed an uncanny co-incidence to me that significant gold nuggets were always found in Victoria's Golden Triangle just prior to the Christmas, Easter and school-term holidays. One such nugget was found west of Bendigo and in a local hotel the celebrations waxed long into the night.

The nugget was displayed on the bar for all to admire while the finder, his eloquence, growing stronger with each glass of beer thrust on him by envious admirers, seemed to stumble in his story and began talking about having been given the nugget.

With a conjurer's swiftness his mates whisked him from the hotel and he was not seen again for several months. The curious sequel came in the analysis of the nugget which proved that it had come from a West Australian goldfield.

Now I come to two experiences which placed a good friendship in jeopardy. At the time I was a journalist on the *Bendigo Advertiser* a local country daily newspaper and worked with another journalist, David Horsfall. David is one of those very rare individuals, gentle, genial, kindly and without a harsh word for anyone.

His proity is a byword in all sections of Bendigo as illustrated by his searching throughout Bendigo for one of his cheques for only $2.00 which through a miscalculation had bounced.

When he located it he bought a round of drinks for his mates in the local hotel to celebrate the re-establishment of his good name (if ever it were in doubt!). David, a very competent wordsmith, is a recognised specialist in the field of gold mining, of which he has an encyclopedic knowledge.

However his idea of joy is to jump into his four-wheeled offroad and follow the tracks of last century's explorers across Australia's deserts.

While the thought of heat, flies, desert salt pans and the stoney gribber plains fill me with horror, they merely bring a happy smile of reminiscence and anticipation to David. Working alongside of me it was inevitable that David would become intrigued with my possessing of gold nuggets on a Friday and having to return them to Bendigo Mining on the following Monday.

One Monday morning before I could return the nugget David saw me wrapping it tenderly in a piece of plastic. *"Give it to me and I'll put you to a test,"* he said

I groaned inwardly, both from having to preform once again in front groaned inwardly, both from having to perform once again in front of a sceptic and that the nugget was a cool $400. I was told to retire to the nearest lavatory and not to return for five minutes during which time David intended to hide the nugget.

After having used my incarceration to good purpose I returned to the reporters' room.

"You're on your own," said David with a disbelieving grin. Feeling a bit silly standing in such a den of cynicism as a reporters' room holding a bent wire and having an expert in gold mining leaning back watching me I set about my task. But nothing happened.

No matter which way I turned the wire was unresponsive. To say I was getting flustered was putting it middly. Once again I had failed - a fact which would bring hilarity to the other dozen or so literary non-believers when they arrived at work. *"How about I turn off the computers ?"* said David*"Anything! Anything!" I thought*.

Off went the bank of some 25 computers and immediately the wire swung aroud. It began pointing to a heap of discarded newspapers and at once I realised I had really failed.

With increasing dread I moved over the papers and once over them the wire swung violently sideways.

"That's it, a wash-out," I thought, adding aloud, *"Sorry, Dave, it's the best I can do."* Dave leapt to his feet and emitted his favourite expression. *"By Jove,"* he exclaimed. *"You've done it!"*

He jumped across the room and thrust his hand into the heap and brought forth the gleaming nugget. Relief, relief, relief.

I grabbed the nugget and sped across to Bendigo Mining and swapped it for my IOU before any further tests crossed his mind.

However Dave, a wily bird, had more in store for me. At lunch time several of us retired to a nearby hotel. After quenching our thirst David filled a lull in the conversation with this announcement: *"Listen to what Richard did this morning."*

As the tale unfolded I pushed my face deeper and deeper into my pot of ale wishing to disappear out of sight beneath its froth. There was open amazement, which switched immediately to exclamations of total disbelief. *"Give us a demonstration,"* I heard on all sides.

At that time I used to carry a gold-plated 20-cent coin with me to use in experiments in place of a nugget. *"Give me the coin and go outside into the street,"* said Dave. *"If he can't find the coin then he pays for our beer,"* were the last words I heard.

Much was at stake. It was a lonely few minutes outside in the street before I was recalled and had to produce my wire. Mingling sweat with my with my prayers I stood in the centre of the barroom hoping something would happen. It did. The wire swung around and pointed immediately at the barman. *"It seems to be over in that direction,"* was all I could say, a little foolishly.

There was dead silence in the bar as the trapdoor to the cellar under where the barman had stood was open and the coin was found on a ledge. The beer was on them but if nothing else it proved a beer in the hand is worth a nugget in the bush!

By now the reader must be asking why my mate and I persisted in trying to find gold over such a long period. Firstly it must be understood that the entire Golden Triangle had been dug over many times since the 1850s and that recently it had been combed by a new army of propectors armed with electronic metal detectors.

We knew our chances of success were exceedingly slim but as we progressed in our search we tried out many new divining techniques, several of which were later used successfully in other applications. Between the two of us we created a variety of divining wires including L-wires with tiny parabolas on the ends. One such wire was so sensitive that it could indicate radiation sources up to 100 kilometres away.

Also like all experimenters there was the stimulus of knowing we were trying to extend a relatively new frontier of science. The fact that our laboratory was the beautiful Australian bush played no mean part in it. Looking back I would say that the introduction of surveying techniques into remote map divining was an outstanding achievement as it raised it to a new level of accuracy.

Being able to locate gold reefs with ease held us on a razor's edge of expectation of finding surface gold which would have compensated us for all our hard work. Our gold reef expertise was commercially valueless as we did not have the money to finance a high-cost mining venture and at the time the gold-mining industry was dormant through its output.

One of our most notable failures in divining was trying to pick horse-race results and lottery numbers, but then this was not unexpected because of our pecuniary interest. However it did provide an excuse for many a quick trip into the nearest town and a brief call at a local pub.

One interesting and fortunately successful experiment was forced on me. I had been driving around in the bush a few kilometres out of the small township of Tarnagulla, west of Bendigo, when a very thick mist rolled in reducing visibility to about three metres. The area was criss-crossed by so many tracks that it was impossible to choose which one led to the highway, only about two kilometres away.

First I drew on my Boy Scout training and tried to find a tree with moss on the back to ascertain the direction of north. But none was apparent on any tree. Of course, the answer lay in using divining skills to find north, but I'd left my wire and pendulum somewhere in the grass and couldn't find them. Then came a bright idea - why not make a pendulum which finally swung eagerly in the direction of north consisted of an old spark plug tied to a long strand of sugar grass.

The upshot was that I found our way out of the bush and immediately retired to the Golden Age Hotel in nearby Tarnagulla for sustenance. This little pub was most deceptive as the splendour of its name was in contrast to the building's modest and faded Victorian facade. The public bar was small, more like a much-used drawing room and its bar could not be fronted by more than a dozen people at the one time.

Small and a little dowdy as it was the pub's cliam to fame stretched far and wide across Victoria as on its wall was a collection of photographs of successful gold seekers, each with one grubby paw holding a nugget of eye-widening size while in the other was a much-sipped glass of beer.

Slightly glazed and beaming faces of the bucolic owners of these hands leered triumphantly back into the bar to the agonising envy of the patrons.

The picture gallery was a great stimulus to drinking as patrons tended to gulp their beer more hurriedly to drown their sorrows for not being able to clutch similar nuggets. Those who have visited this hotel will recall the wall adornments which included a rare musical instrument, a one-stringed *"lavatorium"* made from a toilet seat, an Irish dog carrier made from steel with a nose muzzle at one end and a brace and a bit at the other and, best of all, the remains of an electronic gold detector whose owner had vented his frustration at not finding gold by blasting it with a shotgun. Mute testimony to unsatisfied greed.

Search for an old pub

The National Hotel, Gisborne, Victoria, circa 1885.

The National Hotel, Gisborne, Victoria, circa 1885

The buildings which men and women have erected to live, work and worship are a lasting record of their history. As a diviner living in Australia there has not been much in this field to investigate as the itinerant life of the Aborigines did not include any durable buildings of any type.

However in England shortly after my marriage, my wife, a librarian, was able to obtain a deleted copy of Bannister-Fletcher's *History of Comparative Architecture*, and I was completely hooked. If anyone wants to while away many fascinating hours studying the history of mankind then Bannister Fletcher is an able guide.

My particular interest was Gothic churches, and my many trips to the Continent were what a lot of people superciliously called *"Churching,"* but I didn't care. One interesting fact is that there are very few Gothic churches still in existence which were completed during any one period, most having additions or alterations made over a number of periods.

One such little gem of architectural integrity worth the attention of any person, student, dilettante or tourist interested in buildings is L'Eglise Notre-Dame du Sablon in Brussels. This church, originally built in the 15th century, was completely restored in the Neo-Gothic style towards the end of last century.

The work done by architect Van Ysendijck is considered a masterpiece. I did not think of using divining skills in archeological research until I read of the wonderful work of Jim Scott-Elliott, a retired major-general who lived in Scotland.

A local diviner showed him how to use both wire and pendulum and from that moment he began a second and just as illustrious career as an amateur archaeologist. It is sad that like so many other diviners this dedicated man had to battle continually with officialdom to have his methods of research and finds accepted. But nothing deterred him - what would one have expected from a person of proven courage and ability, and eventually he produced a remarkable book on his methods and achievements, *Dowsing: One Man's Way.* Here is an extract from an address to the 1973 convention of the American Society for Dowsers:

> *"The generation that I belong to is sceptical and always asks for proof that dowsing works. On the other hand, the young are open and prepared to 'have a try' and use it. Officialdom of all kinds does not accept it. Nor does science, though we have a number of scientists and geologists in our British Society of Dowsers.*
>
> *It is essential that we, as dowsers, overcome this barrier of officialdom, and I believe we can only do this by successful*

results. To achieve this I suggest we must cut out inefficient dowsing as far as possible, and so demonstrate by accurate work by qualified dowsers, that dowsing not only works but can be useful and in a money-mad world, a saver of time, labour and money. So, may I urge that we expect from the qualified dowser an outlook that expects nothing short of success - not boastfully but humbly - based on a quiet acceptance of an ability, gifted to us, but developed by hard work and trained in the harsh field of experience where success and failure mean much to one's professional integrity."

As a diviner my flirtation with archaeology came when the site of an old hotel public house near Gisborne in Central Victoria was about to be obliterated by an advancing highway by-pass.

The site was of particular historical value as the pub had been one of the stopping places for diggers on their way to the Bendigo goldfields farther north. It adjoined a swampy area so water was always available for the thirsty travellers. As many had carts and barrows which needed urgent repairs it was not long before a smity set up his forge.

Eventually the pub, made of local basalt, was erected to provide a more popular type of thirst quencher. The building was demolished early this century and the land became part of a farm.

My friend, Tony Foster, also a diviner, who lived near Gisborne, invited me to check the site with him as a archaeologist was trying to locate the hotel's cellars. We went to the site and with a tape made an accurate plan of it, including a few features such as the floor of the smithy's forge and the pub's groundwater tank.

Back home at Bendigo I made a large-scale plan of the site, using an original map to which I added our measurements, and then set to work with a small pendulum to see if I could find the two cellars. This seemed comparatively easy, but the doubt in my mind was the length of the building which the pendulum indicated was about 40 metres.

I rang Tony who said he had got about the same length, a fact which we were able to confirm on a second visit to the site where we found that more of the building's foundations had been excavated. With our confidence boosted by getting the building's length right we then examined the various basement walls which also had been revealed and found that the two cellars were where we had located them by divining.

Next came a most difficult drawing which I had only attempted twice before in oil divining - an elevation. In one instance I drew up a geological elevation of an oil search area and found it compared favourably with a normal seismic readout. However I had never attempted to do an elevation of a building.

So it was with some trepidation I began the task and on completion came up with the edifice on the next page. Eventually I was able to compare it with a photocopy of an early photograph of the hotel which is also shown

Having seen this photocopy I did not try to make an enlargement of my drawing for the first glance would have programmed my mind as to what any further divined result would be.

I am the first to agree that this instance of archeological divining could be deemed as another the case of 'One swallow does not making a spring,' and that it pales when compared with the brilliance of Jim Scott Elliott's achievements. However to me it is another indication of the extent and variety of purposes to which divining can be applied.

Search for National Hotel, Gisborne

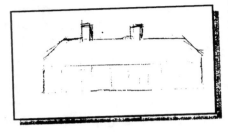

First divining sketch of the pub's facade after being told its approximate position. Tony Foster visited the site and found the foundations had been uncovered. He confirmed our estimates as to the pub's position and it's length.

The perimeter of the pub as measured by Tony and myself after more excavating had been done. We divined the position of the two cellars which are shown on the sketch and later found to be correctly

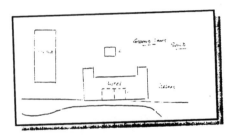

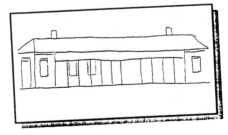

My further attempt at divining the facade. At this stage neither Tony nor I had seen an old photograph of the pub which had been passed to an archaeologist. A photostat of this photograph is at the start of this chapter.

Through a glass, darkly...

Can human beings see into the future? The arguments for and against have raged on for thousands of years and as yet there is no resolution. Socrates described prophesy as a *"madness which is the special gift of heaven."* In other words he took a $1.00 bet each way without committing himself.

If we look at famous and infamous prophets in the past 2,000 odd years there is a disturbing ring of truth about their pronouncements. Most of them, ranging from the Pythia of Delphi and Nostradamus to Dr Dee and Mrs Jean Dixon, undoubtedly had the ability to read the future but unfortunately when this deserted them they added their own embellishments, which just as often did not occur, thereby casting doubt on everything they said.

However there have been occasions when prophesies have proven correct which opens up a massive can of scientific worms about the nature of the cosmos in which we live. The ability of people to prophesy underscores that immortal paragraph in the 1 Corinthians 13:

> *"For now we see through a glass darkly;*
> *but then face to face:*
> *now I know in part;*
> *but then I shall know even as also I am known."*

Prophesy is the hand-maiden of clairvoyance and sometimes when I was working with Jill Foster I became aware that instead of talking about a specific incident in the past she was in fact unconsciously referring to the future. At times I thought her occasional references to what would happen were pure coincidental but the more I knew her the greater became my belief that at times she could indeed see through that glass darkly.

Before relating some cases of prophesy which have proven correct I would suggest that anyone who is totally opposed to prophesy should potter along to their nearest library and consult Von Nostrand's *Scientific Encyclopedia*, which must rate as one of the most incredible compendiums of man's practical knowledge ever printed.

If the reader accepts, as the greatest of today's scientists do, that the entire cosmos is composed of nothing more than energy of various forms, then they should look up Von Nostrand's entry on this subject.

It occupies only three pages out of a total of 2,300, and begins with Einstein's Theory of Relativity and his omnipotent and omniscient formula $E = MC2$, which shows that matter and time are interrelated facets of energy. This is followed by Planck's Quantum theory which holds that energy radiation is made up of definite quanta or increments of energy proportional to frequency, density or radiation. Ahead of those pronouncements nobody has come up with the answer to what energy is.

When Einstein was asked what he thought energy was he said: "*I don't know what it is, but it's there, let's use it.*" (I hope the reader will forgive me repeating this statement).

Also one of the basic laws of the behaviour of energy is that it can never be destroyed; it can only be converted into some other form of energy, eloquently and tragically proven by the destruction of Nagasaki and Hiroshima in 1945. This law is known generally as the Law of the Conservation of Energy.

154

It must follow, therefore, as time is part of energy and energy cannot be destroyed, only converted, then the entire energy which constitutes the cosmos and everything in it, has always existed, exists now and will continue to exist, albeit in different forms at different times. If this is so then prophesy must be seen simply as the ability of a person to tune into energy forms and relationships not yet recognised by human consciousness. This view casts an interesting light on re-incarnation but that is another topic.

The mixture of clairvoyance and divining was demonstrated eloquently by Capt Vo Sum of the South Vietnamese Navy who, at the age of seven, had been taught to use a pendulum to obtain answers by his father using a pendulum on a question and answer basis. He was present when his father began the heart-breaking search with a pendulum for Vo Sum's brother who went missing in the war.

By watching the pendulums movements his father concluded that his son become ill in Marseille in Southern France where he eventually died. Tragically this was confirmed some years later. Using only an ebony ball attached to a string Vo Sum played a significant role in helping to locate missing South Vietnamese prisoners of war.

Vo Sum outstanding ability as a yes-no diviner was demonstrated during the war when he was an intership communications officer. He located a raft carrying the crew of a disabled patrol boat by merely posing questions and relying on his pendulum to give the right answers.

His unique ability resulted in his being seconded to naval headquarters where he was giving the job of trying to track down a junk carrying a large shipment of opium believed to have been loaded at the Thai port of Satahip.

After getting a positive answer from the pendulum that he should work on the problem - clockwise gyrations - Vo Sum began a series of questions relating to the future movements of the junk and the time and place it would be apprehended.

He even predicted the exact time the searching party would locate the contraband hidden in sealed containers in a storage tank and the subsequent arrest of the junk's captain. This well-documented case is related in Christopher Bird's book, "*Divining*".

A noted clairvoyant in Bendigo is Maureen Dalzeal, of White Hills. I became fascinated with her ability as a mental telepathist and clairvoyant, and talked with her on several occasions. When I first met her she did not know I was a diviner, and in answer to a question about my future she said: "*I see you travelling on a long road on one side of which is water. Your future is tied up with water.*"

On the way home in the car I could not get her comment out of my mind and I began think of all the long roads on one side of which was either the sea or a lake. I puzzled over this many times in the next year or two but nothing came to mind. One possibility was the Great Ocean Road in Victoria which overlooks Bass Strait but somehow I knew this was wrong.

One day I was working on the mundane job of weeding my rose garden when I suddenly understood what Maureen had meant. The long road was my life and the water concerned my growing study of water divining.

Some year's later at Port Fairy I worked on the beach adjoining Bass Strait, divining for the lost wreck of the famous Mahogany Ship, and also have spent considerable time divining for oil in the same waters. Co-incidence.

Maureen used to hold what she called "*Over-the-Top*" sessions of clairvoyance when she would work give readings for six or seven people. I attended a few of these sessions and on one occasion she began by closing her eyes in concentration for a minute or so then opened them and looked directly at a young woman sitting next to her. *"When I look at you all I see ahead is darkness. You will be surrounded by darkness. Can you suggest why I should feel this way?"*

The young woman looked a little embarrassed at being the centre of attention. *"Perhaps it's because I haven't paid the power bill,"* she said. When the laughter had died down Maureen looked over towards where I was sitting on a couch between two women and with a frown said:

"Someone on that couch is pregnant." I immediately put up my hand and said: *"It's not me."* The two women also denied having conceived but then another woman leaning against the end of the couch said: *"It's me. I was told this afternoon."* In this case Maureen seemed to have switched from prophesy to clairvoyance or mental telepathy.

In my own case one experience gave me pause to think. On one particular day I caught the Eaglehawk bus in Bendigo at 4 pm not so long ago and showed the driver my wallet which contained my return ticket.

When I got to my flat I felt for my wallet but it was not in my pocket. Thinking I was becoming absent minded I searched the flat but to no avail. There wasn't much money in the wallet but it contained a bridgehand of plastic cards which are such a nuisance to replace. I was sitting sitting at my desk when I posed the question: *"In which direction is my wallet?"*

The result was frustrating as the pendulum oscillated in one direction then switched to another. A useless result. Then I remembered where the optimum divining position in my flat was - every diviner should establish this with his or her pendulum - and when I repeated the question and the pendulums movement pointed immediately and quite definitely towards Bendigo.

Then I asked a series of questions which included:

Did I leave it on the bus ?	- Yes
Did it slip out of my pocket onto the seat ?	- No
On to the floor ?	- Yes
Is it still in the bus ?	- Yes
Has it been handed to the bus driver ?	- Yes
Will I get it back intact ?	- Yes
Today or tomorrow ?	- Today
At what time ?	- At 6.30 pm

Realising I could be emotionally involved in the loss of the wallet I was very sceptical about the answers I'd received to my questions but I thought they were worth checking out. I rang the bus company and ascertained when the bus would return to Eaglehawk. On meeting the bus driver at 6.30 pm, Bill, handed my wallet to me, saying: *"This is your lucky day."*

Did I, like Vo Sum and Maureen, momentarily see through that dark glass and see the future? I wonder.

I have related this experience of the lost wallet merely to show another aspect in which divining can be applied in the search for a lost article. In this case it may well be asked how was I successful when I was emotionally envolved in the outcome of the quest.

In actual fact in this particular case I remember being quite offhand about whether or not the wallet turned up. There was not much money in it and the only problem if it were lost was the replacement of a few plastic cards.
As Maureen would say: *"I'll leave it with you."* Of course, as proof of the ability to foresee the future, I realise this incident is unacceptable.

Earlier, when I was dealing with negative telluric vibrations it was suggested that in addition to areas where negative vibrations were congested and damaging there could be areas which contributed to a diviner's ability to perform. At the time I thought this was a load of rubbish, such was my scepicicism even to divining, but nevertheless I conducted a series of experiments to ascertain if there were any truth in it.

All I can relate is that I do seem to be able to divine more accurately in certain places in my rooms. Again, this is an area for investigation. In this I recall Vo Sum's comment that when he was engaged heavily in looking for lost people in Vietnam he made a practice of working in the early hours of the morning when there were no extraneous influences which could affect his divining ability.

On many occasions I have done the same and have found that some of my best results have occurred about this time. Also I now make it a practice of having a notepad and pen beside the bed for I find that early in the morning in that wonderful nebulous twilight between waking and sleep enlightening ideas often pop into my head which are difficult to remember as later I grope for a cup of coffee.

Did Jesus visit Tibet and India ?

The distinguished British historian, H.G. Wells, described Siddhartha Gautama, better known as the Buddha, as "*The greatest man who ever lived.*" Wells, who used to mix with T.H.Huxley and Bernard Shaw, was regarded as one of the greatest novelist-philosophers of his day, so who am I, a mere tram ticket under the shoe soles of such great ones, to disagree?

But once again, here I am, charging in where angels would never go. To me, a person quite equal to the Buddha was Jesus of Nazareth.

The Buddha's philosophy was based on achieving happiness through overcoming desire, acceptance of cause and effect and the wisdom of compassion to all others and things. However Jesus brought a devastingly simple philosophy to the savage Roman world which not only was largely instrumental in its demise but created a new religion based on Judaism. His teaching was:

Love for one another as we love ourselves.

It is interesting that the famous jurist and founder of the British Buddhist Society, Christmas Humphreys, said the entire Buddhist philosophy could be described by the teachings of Jesus.

Although not much of a theist, I have always been fascinated with the life of Jesus, and a couple of years ago while divining on a map of the Middle East I fell to wondering where did Jesus go between the ages of about 12 and 30 years when he is not mentioned in the Christian scriptures. Beginning at Jerusalem I allowed the pendulum to swing where it liked and to my surprise it went north-east to where it joined the Grand Silk Road to China from where it branched down through Tibet to India, Sri Lanka, Burma, and then back to India, the Arabian Peninsula and Jerusalem.

My interest in this exploration, begun so casually, became intense when the pendulums movements carried it along the Silk Road to an obscure settlement in Turkmenskaj midway between Tehran and Samarakand. It's name? Mary. What obscure reason did remote, itinerant desert tribes have for giving their meeting place the same name of Jesus' mother? Was it deliberate, chance or was I creating something out of nothing? Perhaps this could be followed up.

Bach flower remedies

Herbal remedies for illness have been used by mankind since long before he lifted his knuckles off the ground. Knowledge about the beneficial properties of plants are known to many animals and one has only to study a dog or cat which often resorts to chewing a piece of grass when its diet is deficient or it is unwell. Its action is far from stupid for one has only to reflect that after 18 months of eating grass a tiny calf turns into a massive bullock.

Chinese medicine is largely based on herbal medicine whose origin are lost in time. There is a tendency in the West for doctors to look askance at such herbal treatments but then many of our most effective drugs have been synthesised from herbs. They include digitalis and quinidine, heart drugs, tubocurarine, a muscle relaxant, and morphine and codeine, anaesthetics.

While both Eastern and Western medicine have this similarity, there is a fundamental difference between them in the approach to illness. In the East the doctor is concerned principally with what makes a person ill while his Western colleague who tends to concentrate on treating the symptoms of disease.

Early in the 1930s in Harley Street, London, where the doyen of the British medical profession still hang out their shingles, one particular doctor became increasingly concerned that many diseases could in themselves be symptoms of more deep-seated malaises. His name was Edward Bach. The question which kept plaguing him was why should a person become ill in the first place? With the advanced medical knowledge, skills and equipment of the day doctors were increasingly able to identify the diseases which resulted in the symptoms, but why the human body should become prey to the diseases in the first place was still unknown.

To Dr Bach it seemed the answer might lie in the innermost core of the human entity which in essence was a reflection of the wider harmony of the cosmos of which it was a part. He reasoned that if disease, which was treatable by herbal remedies, was a reflection of a basic discord of the inner-being, then perhaps there were herbal remedies which could assist in bringing the inner-being back into a state of harmony where in the disease did not exist.

In these days of gurus for everything - from understanding re-incarnation, diagnosing motor-vehicle faults and curing back-ache by belly dancing - one is apt to think *"Oh, so gurus existed in the 1930s as well."* But hold a moment. This doctor was no five-week wonder. Here are his qualifications: MB, BS, MRCS, LRCP, DPH (Camb.).

The time came when the problem weighed so heavily on Dr Bach that he gave up his lucrative practice and began a line of scientific research which was to revolutionise the medical approach to curing disease.

After many years of work which involved testing the sun-heat distillation of many thousands of plants he eventually identified 38 which could restore the inner harmony of a person suffering from disease and thus rid them of the very basis of that disease.

His system, which became this great man's epitaph, is called simply *"The Bach Flower Remedies."* His benediction was this:

"Let not the simplicity of this method deter you from its use, for you will find the further your researches advance, the greater you will realise the simplicity of all Creation.

Take no notice of the disease; think only of the outlook on life of the one in distress.

Final and complete healing will come from within, from the soul itself, which by his beneficence radiates harmony throughout the personality when allowed to do so"

I was introduced to Bach Flower Remedies by a diviner, Jill Foster, of Eaglehawk, near where I live. Jill is an intriguing person who prescribes the remedies by running her a pendulum down the list of 38 different flower essences and then selecting them according to the pendulums movement.

I'd always been interested in the remedies and why they worked and when I heard that she was a pendularist, I quickly made an appointment to see her. Here is what happened:

We sat down on either side of the kitchen table and after we had clasped our left hands diagonally across the table, she picked up a small pendulum with her right hand while in my right hand I held a pen poised to write on a small pad.

After a brief moment of concentration Jill began moving the pendulum down the remedy list watching it oscillate over each one. Suddenly the pendulum began to gyrate over one particular remedy and Jill asked to write it down.

Twice more the same thing happened and when she finished and returned the pendulum to its pouch, she produced three small bottles of the remedies named from a large box.

She took four drops of each remedy from its bottle and injected them into a larger bottle containing distilled water and a teaspoonful of brandy. This she shook up then taking an eyedropper she extracted 10 drops from the mixture which I placed in my mouth.

Ever the sceptic I asked why I should take them as there was nothing wrong with me. Jill merely said that the pendulum had indicated my inner being required the benefit of these particular herbs. Small talk followed then, armed with a book on Bach Flower Remedies, I left and, good humored, began taking the required dose which had to be taken four times a day.

I had been incorrect in stating that there was nothing wrong with me as my sleeping pattern of previous weeks had been abnormal - dozing for an hour, reading for four-to five hours, followed by three hours of heavy sleep which left me tired, tense and often depressed. The following morning I awoke and could not believe the clock - I had slept for eight hours and felt zipping with energy.

Over the next few days my new sleeping pattern continued and as did my new energy level. This triggered me to begin ringing around people who had taken the Bach Flower Remedies and I was amazed to hear that most had had similar experiences and in many cases the disease from which they suffered had either recessed or been cured. These successes mirrored the many cases histories which had been published by the doctor and later by many of his disciples.

The following week I asked Jill why she used a pendulum to select remedies and she replied that she preferred this method rather than trying to diagnose the state of a person's inner harmony by observing their behaviour. Her many successes with Bach Flower Remedies are typical of the effectiveness of this procedure. It is obvious to the reader that I am now a confirmed believer in the use of Bach Flower Remedies to help overcome the fundamental causes of illness, that is, why human beings become susceptible to disease in the first place. Having studied Jill at work several times on a variety of projects I am convinced she is a clairvoyant and uses a pendulum as a symbolic expression of her intuition.

Also I regard Jill's use of a pendulum to identify remedies needed by a person as further evidence of divining being a symbolic expression of the ability of the subconscious mind to communicate selectively with other sources of information. It is interesting that Bach Flower Remedies have been used successfully even to restore animals and plants to health.

How to use Bach Flower Remedies

Bach Flower Remedies are available from most health stores.
It is suggested you obtain a list of the remedies and pass a pendulum slowly across each of the main headings to establish which group could apply either to yourself or another person.
Do the same with each remedy in the group selected.
The recommended dossage of remedies is four drops each mixed recommended dossage of remedies is four drops of each mixed with 0.3 ml of pure water to which one teaspoonful of brandy has been handed.Consume or apply as recommended, which is usually about 10 drops of the mixture four times daily.

Tracing a Maori voyage

One day when talking to Jill she said: "*You were a Maori in a previous life.*" I glanced quickly at her but she wasn't joking. When a person who has proven themselves to be a medium makes a flat statement like that it bears investigating even by a dedicated sceptic.

Jill is not like the usual medium who dips into a mystical Encyclopedia Britannica and spouts information like the famous American, Edgar Cayce. For a brief time she actually becomes a person in a past life and expresses how they felt emotionally at a particular time. To say I was intrigued is a colossal understatement as I have always been intensely interested in Maoris, their history and their culture.

I sailed with a Maori, Roger Tahere Delamere Dansey, on the troopship, the MV Duntroon after World War 2 and later shared a flat with him in the Melbourne suburb of Brighton. We met under unusual circumstances. I'd just joined the ship and was directed to a cabin which had to be shared by six men.

This room at the Savoy was empty at the time and I recall wondering what sort of hell-hole it would be sardined with five other sweaty blokes in the tropics. Just as I dumped my gear on an empty lower bunk a hearty chuckle reverberated from overhead.

Seeking the origin of these sounds of happiness, I pulled back the curtains which enclosed the top bunk. I was greeted by a happy smiling Buddha who waved a small blue-covered book at me, saying: *"You must read this. It'll kill you."* It was the *Decameron* of Giovanni Boccaccio, an anthology of immortal tales only equalled in *The Canterbury Tales* by Chaucer.

In Chaucer the tales are often boring but in Boccaccio, while the tellers sometimes drag the chain, their stories never do as they are full of wit, spice and belly laughs. And it was a series of belly laughs which were coming from the upper bunk, the occupant of which was Roger Tahere Delamere Dansey. During the subsequent voyage he and I formed a close friendship which lasted long after we had left the ship.

Roger's wartime exploits deserve a book on their own - he fought with the Maori Battalion and flew with the RAF. Before the war he was in Berlin for the 1936 Olympics Games. Recalling this he said: *"Anyone who had seen the Blackshirts strutting about in their jackboots would have realised they were itching for war. Not being of pure Aryan blood they tried to provoke me a couple of times but I'd been warned not to mix it with them. No Pakeha has ever treated me like that before or since."*

Another close friend of mine had been a Maori clarinet player who had taken up music after serving an apprenticeship as a Maori doctor. It was he who told me that the Maoris used leaf mould for healing wounds long before the British microbiologist, Alexander Fleming was knighted for its discovery.

The next time I saw Jill I took with me a map of New Zealand and asked if she would help me try to locate the origin of the Maoris' Polynesian ancestors. I proposed that we should combine her skill as a clairvoyant and mine as a diviner and try to trace one of the migratory voyages. The first phase of this research would be to trace an exploratory Polynesian voyage down the coast of the North Island, with the second trying to follow the return journey of a Polynesian canoe back to its place of origin, wherever that might be.

Jill said she knew nothing at all about the Maoris but was interested in ethnic origins as her ancestors were Canadian Indians. I had told Jill I had lived in New Zealand for about two years but I never related how closely my family was associated with the country over two generations.

My father had fought with the Canterbury Mounted Rifles and the NZ Camel Corps in World War1 and my parents were married in Wanganui, where my brother Alan, now a resident of Christchurch, was born.

Because of Jill's total ignorance of the subject we were to investigate I considered any result met an initial criteria of acceptance.

On the day we began we went to her front room which she called her "*quiet room.*" She called it that because she required peace and quiet to attain the high meditative state for prescribing Bach Flower Remedies.

The room, which was sparsely furnished, had a strange effect on me. Within minutes I could feel the silence. It was if the raucous, discordant, mechanical world outside no longer existed and I had stepped through a looking glass into another existence. Jill and I sat quietly until our minds had adjusted to each other, then she indicated she was ready to begin.

I had brought with me a map of New Zealand which I laid on the small table between us. We held our left hands diagonally across the map and I held a pencil in my right hand. I asked Jill, who had closed her eyes, where the first Polynesian canoe had landed and began to move the pencil down the coastline beginning at North Cape in the North Island. As the point moved southwards Jill began describing her emotional reactions. She was calm until the pencil got to Tauranga when she clenched her fingers around mine and drew back. She said; "*There is death there, a massacre. I'm frightened.*"

Glancing up I saw her face was screwed up in fear. She was not acting, and at the same time I felt distinctly uneasy. As the pencil continued down the coast she appeared to relax, and on reaching Hawkes Bay she said felt a tingling in her body.

"*I like this place,*" she said. As the pencil continued to move farther down the coast she became increasingly tense, and complained of feeling cold and depressed. "*I feel lost,*" she said.

When the pencil point rounded Cape Pallister and moved into Cook Strait, she panicked and clutched my hand until it hurt. "*I'm frightened, I'm frightened,*" she cried out, and then at Arapawa Island she almost shouted: "*We must turn back, the sea is terrible, we can't go any further.*"

By now Jill was so visibly distressed I back-tracked the pencil and as it rounded the cape again and headed north she relaxed. This ended the first phase of our research. I then proposed that we should try to find where the Polynesians had made a temporary settlement to prepare for the journey home - wherever that might be. At once she indicated Hawkes Bay, and I moved the pencil in towards Haumoana. "*That's it, that's the place,*" she said, adding, "*It's good to relax again.*"

The next step was to try to retrace the Polynesians voyage back to their home island. In this experiment I intended to use a pendulum rather than a pencil as an indicator. Firstly, I drew a line north to south down the map about 1,500 kilometres east of New Zealand then while Jill sat with her eyes closed I began moving the pendulum down the line trying to pick up the track of the canoe where it crossed, that is of course, if it did go this way. Suddenly the pendulum began to swing sideways.

As a diviner I believed I had found the course of some vessel or other. I asked her how she felt. "*Oh, I feel so full of energy,*" she exclaimed. "*This is exciting.*"

I marked the place on the line and went farther south but her reactions were negative. Next, using a long rule I connected the mark on the line with Haumoana, and extended a straight line across the Pacific. It ended in the Society Islands, south of Tahiti, which is believed to be the legendary island of Havaiki, the origin of an ancient migration to Hawaii.

Moving the pendulum back to Haumoana I began to move it along the ruled track and Jill gave a running commentary of her feelings which included happiness, misapprehension, energy, warmth but never sadness, fear or horror. I realised that a canoe voyage would never have proceeded in a straight line but then as we were both in such a high state of awareness, this physical limitation ceased to apply. When the pendulum neared the Society Islands Jill made me stop. *"There seems to be an argument, a great argument going on,"* she said. *"People are shouting at each other, they don't know which way to go."*

I had read of the religious intolerance of the ancient Polynesian people in these islands and I wondered if the New Zealand migrations had been triggered by a similar impetus.

Next I obtained a book of Maori legends and drew up a list of names to put to Jill, which I did without recounting the legends to her. The first three names were Toi, Whatonga and Turahai. She studied the names for some time then said the first, Toi, made her feel very sad. *"I get the feeling of being lost and spread out,"* she said. *"I feel I'm waiting, longing for something or someone."*

Then I told her of the ancient legend of the great Polynesian chief, Toi, who set out to find his grandsons, Whatonga and Turahai, whose canoe had been washed out to sea in a great storm. The search led Toi far from his home over vast stretches of ocean until he landed in New Zealand where he joined a group of Polynesians at Whakatane.

Meanwhile the two grandsons returned home and on finding their grandfather gone, set out to search for him and eventually they were reunited at Whakatane. Toi and his grandsons and their crews settled permanently in the North Island where later they were joined by several other migrations.

On returning to my home, Jill's remark that her forebears had originally been Canadian Indians had me reaching for a large map of Canada. I ran my pendulum down the west coast and asked the question: where was Jill's family home?

The pendulum began oscillating towards the east and I followed its direction across the Rockies to the Winnipeg area where it began gyrating. I showed the map to Jill and the small area I had marked south of Winnipeg. *"We are hiding,"* she said. *"There are guns. They are searching for us. It's the French. Oh, I don't like them. We must escape."* Jill was silent for a moment then opening her eyes she went on: *"We lived near a big lake not far away. They had guns."*

I moved the pendulum over a large map of the Province of Manitoba and when it got to the town of Dauphin on the western shore of Lake Manitoba it again gyrated. *"This is it. This was my home and now they have stolen it."* she said.

In the history of Canada the French were often in conflict with the Indians, who bitterly opposed their invasion, and later the French supported Huron Indians in a bloody war against the Iroquois. Were Jill's forbears involved in this conflict? It is odd that the town bears the traditional name given to the eldest son of a French king.

I have recounted these tentative experiments to show yet another field in which I believe it is possible to use divining to unravel the mysteries of time. Perhaps other more sensitive diviners working with clairvoyants might similarly combine their skills and arrive at a much more precise understanding of aspects of the past.

172

Searching for lost ships

In November, 1941, Australians opened their newspapers to read that the HMAS Sydney was missing and that the fate of the 645 crew was unknown.

Australia was stunned by the news. The Sydney, the biggest and most powerful ship in the Australian fleet, had only recently returned to Australia after winning glory in the Mediterranean conflict.

Some three days before the announcement, when the Sydney could not be raised by radio, a preliminary search was organised. When she was not sighted one of the biggest air and sea hunts in Australia's history was mounted.

But all was in vain. No sign of the Sydney, not even one piece of identifiable wreckage or debris, was every found.

The whole nation went into mourning.

News about the fate of the Sydney came from the first of 240 German sailors from the notorious raider, the Kormoran, who were rescued about 100 miles off Carnarvon. They reported that their vessel had been involved in a fierce action with the Sydney which had been badly damaged and was last seen heading south-east on fire.

The story told by the German survivors when interrogated was that the Sydney had challenged the Kormoran to give a secret recognition signal but the raider replied with a broadside from its battery of six-inch guns catching the Sydney completely unawares. In the ensuing battle which lasted 30 minutes both vessels sustained critical damage, each having been hit many times. Eventually the Kormoran was hit by one of Sydney's torpedoes and broke in two.

The search for the Sydney continued for several days afterwards but the only thing found was an empty Carley survival float some 120 miles north-west of Carnarvon. Nearby was an unexplained circular patch of linseed oil. Neither was identified.

Through the ineptness of the Australian naval command, the German survivors were permitted to gather together before being interrogated, and after the war it was found that the German officers had instructed their men to give confusing and misleading stories about the action.

No doubt this was motivated by the fear of what might happen to them if they reported that when last seen the Sydney was ablaze from stem to stern and most likely blew up, as did the HMS Hood earlier in the war.

Several investigations were held into the loss of the Sydney but all differ in their findings. The map showing the navy's official reconstruction of the battle is opposite. However as it is based on the evidence of the crew of the Kormoran it is very suspect. To this day no one knows the final resting place of either ship.

I raised the loss of the Sydney with Jill Foster, who had migrated to Australia after World War 2 but she, not having heard about a warship by that name, thought I was referring to the capital of New South Wales. Jill studied a photograph of the ship for a few minutes. She said; "*What a sad ship, I would not have sailed on her, those poor sailors, what a terrible lesson they had to learn.*"

I am uncertain whether this comment came from her belief that people are reincarnated in order to learn some lesson which will assist them in their evolvement towards perfection or whether she was referring to the futility of war. However, by her comments, it seemed that somehow she tuned into the drama of that fateful day.

Our discussion prompted me to see if it were possible to locate the wrecks of the Sydney and the Kormoran by long-range map divining. As I had not searched for a shipwreck by long-range map divining for some years I thought it wise to check my ability by locating a couple of wrecks whose positions were known by others but not by me. I chose the ill-fated New Zealand inter-island ferry, MV Wahine on which I had sailed several times, and the Russian cruise ship, Mikhail Kermonov, which had sunk off the north coast of New Zealand's South Island.

Having lived in Wellington for about six months I knew the harbour of Port Nicholson well and had experienced the storms that sometimes swept in from the west. In my mind's eye I could see the wreckage of the vessel on the eastern side of the harbour opposite to where the city is situated

I sketched a rough outline of the port from memory but to my bewilderment the wreck appeared to be on the western side of the entrance to the harbour. I repeated this exercise with an accurate map of the harbour but the result was the same. Before confirming the position of the Wahine I tried to find the wreck of the Russian cruise liner.

Again I had a preconception of the wreck being towards the western end of Cook Strait, but my divining survey showed it to be near Cape Jackson, adjoining Queen Charlotte Sound, towards the eastern part of the strait. Without much confidence I rang the Australian Maritime Safety Authority in Canberra to check my findings but was referred to the Wellington Harbour Board whose Search and Rescue Co-ordinator, Capt. Gibb, told

Loss of HMAS Sydney

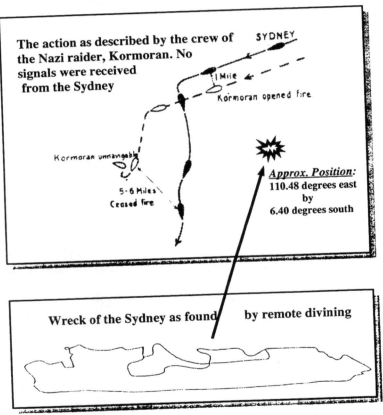

The action as described by the crew of the Nazi raider, Kormoran. No signals were received from the Sydney

SYDNEY

1 Mile

Kormoran opened fire

Kormoran unmanageable

5 - 6 Miles
Ceased fire

Approx. Position:
110.48 degrees east
by
6.40 degrees south

Wreck of the Sydney as found by remote divining

The profile of the Sydney picked up by remote divining has distortions typical of sonar recordings received from shipwrecks

me the Wahine had sunk after hitting Barrett's Reef at the western entrance to Port Nicholson and that the Mikhail Lermontov had sunk near Cape Jackson. Both my long-range NZ searches appeared to be correct.

As the approximate positions of the Sydney and the Kormoran were about the same distance from my home near Bendigo I now felt fairly confident about beginning a long-range divining search for these two vessels.

The following maps show how I approached the search, the result of which seems to show that the ships sank roughly where the German survivors had indicated. The sketches of the two wrecks I made with the help of a pendulum appear to substantiate that the Sydney did disintegrate through a massive internal explosion and also that the Kormoran broke in two. Also shown is the official Navy version of the action based mostly on the accounts given by the crew of the Kormoran.

It does seem strange to me that the Australian Government has never mounted an intense search for the wreckage of the Sydney, as with today's remote-controlled sonar and television techniques the chances of succeeding are very good. This was proven in the cases of finding the Titanic, and British bulk iron-ore carrier, MV Derbyshire, which was lost with all hands in the Philippine Sea south of Japan about the 9th of September, 1980.

My interest in the Derbyshire stemmed from having a close relative working on bulk iron-ore carriers. On his shore leaves over the years I learned a lot about their construction and behaviour both while being loaded and at sea in heavy weather.

My relative had always taken the risks of a sea-going career with a lightness of spirit which was hard for me to understand. However, the thought that the crew of a fully-laden iron-ore bulk carrier had only about three minutes to abandon ship if she foundered was ever a shadow in my mind.

From our talks here is a summary of the reasons why a bulk carrier can founder:

A : *Corrosion causing a weakening of the ship's structure so that it can no longer support the loads it was originally designed to carry;*

B : *A vessel sailing in a stressed condition due to improper distribution of the cargo.*

C : *Stress resulting from uneven loading and discharging; and*

D : *Poor seamanship in bad weather.*

Apparently it is rare for a ship to go down when only one of the above causes occurs, but when two or more coincide the chance of a disaster rises considerably.

As a diviner with a personal interest in bulk carriers I shouldn't have attempted to search for the Derbyshire but unwisely I ignored the basic rule of divining - not having an emotional involvement in any possible outcome - and even went to the length of obtaining data from Geneva on the official searches for the lost vessel. Needless to say my divining search was a failure.

However, the loss of that vessel preyed on my mind and one day I discussed it at some length with Jill. As always when raising a subject with her I did not give her any background on it as this could influence her reaction. In the case of the Derbyshire all I told her was that it had sunk on the way to Japan. When I wrote down the name MV Derbyshire, she closed her eyes and was silent for a minute or two before speaking. *"Those tremendous waves,"* she said. *"It's so frightening, those poor men. Part of the ship seems to be surfing backwards. Now they are all gone."*

I had the uncanny feeling that she could actually see the ship going down.

One day sitting at my computer I began thinking about the Derbyshire and I jotted down these thoughts. A journalists catharsis, I suppose, but here is what is on file:

A ship's last moments

At the time the heavily laden iron-ore bulk carrier was ploughing into a typhoon in the Philippine Sea, west of Taiwan, enroute for Japan, Massive waves were lifting the bow and washing over the hatches to slam titan hammer-blows against the superstructure.

Exploding sea and spume swept 20 to 30 metres upwards completely blocking the angled windows of the bridge as if they were submerged. The only view was through the centrifugal visor.

Often the bow was completely obscured as the ship heaved and groaned its way at reduced speed into the raging storm. Occasionally the officer of the watch, eyes reddened through staring through the visor, saw glimpses of the nearer hatch covers, but then they were instantly covered by the cascading green water sweeping over the deck. The bow could not be seen.

The Derbyshire had been built some 15 years before to meet the world-wide need for the quick transport of iron-ore for the ever-hungry steel mills of Asia and Europe. In recent times she had begun to show signs of her hard life. The stage had not been reached when shipping companies raised ship safety standards to ensure maintenance of delivery schedules. Although surveys had declared her seaworthy the hidden accumulated defects caused by corrosion, metal fatigue and abnormal stresses brought increasing creaks and groans from the Derbyshire's tired hull.

Leaning against the console the officer of the watch glimpsed the bow rising some 200 metres away and he marvelled that such a steel monster like a fully-laden bulk carrier could flex as the Derbyshire did and not snap in two. But then if she didn't move with the waves the ship would break up.

Several times when she was being loaded he, as first officer, had had to order the shore gang to change the order of filling the hatches because the vessel was being stressed beyond the safety limit. The orders had been resented but, to hell with them. Correct loading was his responsibility. He had had to prevent similar stress limits being exceeded in unloading.

About the condition of the Derbyshire's hull he was uncertain, especially how much cancerous rust had eaten into the steel members, and also the extent to which she had been weakened by bad seamanship - being driven beyond safe speeds to meet schedules. Mentally he shrugged his shoulders. All seamen knew that if a loaded bulk iron-ore carrier foundered they had at best 180 seconds to get off - if they were lucky. Still, soon he might be a captain and switch to a less risky job.

At that moment the visor cleared and he saw it - a monstrous, towering wave, the accumulation of several other massive waves, rise out of nowhere and hit the bow shaking the ship as if she were a small row-boat.

The officer grabbed for the edge of the control console as the ship lurched under the impact. With a momentum of thousands of tonnes the wall of water swept on to hit the accommodation bulkhead with an explosion heard above the screaming wind. Then he felt a second wave strike the bow and he knew this would be the moment of truth for the ship - when its 250,000 tonnes weight would be suspended on the crests of just two waves. He held on and waited. It was an eternity. The ship steadied for a moment then flexed like a long banana. Then he knew. The hull was not coming back.

180

Down below frames and stringers buckled and twisted, turning blue under the enormous torsion. The weakened steel tore and screamed. An enormous wound rent the hull in front of the superstructure and the Derbyshire snapped in two as though it were a piece of kindling wood.

The rear of the vessel, the accommodation and engine-room, tipped up. Like a huge sail the superstructure caught the screaming wind and whole of the rear end of the ship began to surf backwards riding on the crest of another enormous wave.

Meanwhile the forward part of the ship had begun to sink. In seconds it plunged out of sight as if it had never existed, disgorging iron ore from its fractured hatches on the way down to the sea bed thousands of metres below. The accommodation section, the lightest part of the vessel, drifted for a while before it lost its buoyancy and finally sank.

From the moment of the fatal break the crew had no chance. The frenzied storm held them captive in a lurching, twisting steel coffin. Those who had not died through injury quickly drowned. Their tomb is on the sea bed in the Philippine Sea, south of Japan.

The forward part of the Derbyshire was found 13 years later by a side scan sonar search mounted by the International Transport Workers' Federation to confirm a theory that the ship was lost due to a massive structural failure causing it to split in two. The ITF was seeking evidence to compel the UK maritime authorities to re- examine the circumstances of the ship's loss with a view to improving sea safety.

The sonar search submersible's last act was to drop a bronze plaque containing the names of the lost crew near a deck anchor at the bow.

Communicating divining ability by touch

Diviner, Eddie Savige, of St James, Victoria, reported the strange phenomenon of passing on the ability to divine by touching another person. He said a neighbour, Johnny White, asked him to find water on his property and when he did so the neighbour tried but was unsuccessful. Eddie said; *"When I put my hand on his arm the wires reacted immediately,"*

I was present when the boring contractor, Bob Tanner, of Kyneton, tried to divine an underground stream but, having influenza, nothing happened. His wife, who could not divine, tried, but again no result. However, the moment Bob put his hand on her shoulder the wire rod reacted vigorously.

What does it all mean ?

After a lifetime exploring the world of divining one fact seems to emerge again and again. It is that the diviner's intuitive mind seems to be able to receive and interpret energy vibrations from an external source. Also that these vibrations can be received as easily from previous phenomena as those which exist today.

Everything - all life forms and the environments in which they exist, past and present - is composed of energy ranging from subtle spiritual energy to the grosser material forms. The problem with the human conscious mind is that it is a very crude instrument and it has to resort to a variety of symbols in an attempt to express even its own functions let alone what is being done by the intuition.

The diviner's wire and pendulum are merely two such symbols. Accepting that a diviner can receive and interpret some energy vibrations from phenomena, this begs the question as to how it is possible for the diviner to receive vibratory information from the past. Initially this seems impossible but then we are faced with the principle of the conservation of energy, which simply means that the total energy of any isolated system is constant and independent of any changes within the system.

In other words in our cosmos, being such a closed system, no energy can ever be destroyed or created, but must always remain constant. This means that the energy of all phenomena, including all biological energy, has existed since the beginning of time and must continue to exist until the universe ends.

This must mean that reincarnation is a fundamental truth of the existence of mankind. The energy which constituted every person who has lived since the beginning of time still exists in some form or other.

We know that on death the molecular components of our bodies break down into their original form - ashes to ashes, dust to dust - but what of that most subtle of all energies, the human spirit?

Is it unreasonable and unrealistic to conclude that spiritual energy obeys the same principle of the conservation of energy? If it does then we co-exist in a cosmos with all those who have lived in the past, and also, as it is impossible to create energy, then with all future beings also.

If we turn to theology then we find that the Christian religion is based on the principle of reincarnation - the resurrection of Jesus of Nazareth.

In the East, Buddhism is also based on reincarnation, with the present Dalai Lama being considered the reincarnation of the Buddha of compassion, Avalokiteshvara.

A few years ago I met a lama who had been declared by no lesser person than the Dalai Lama to be the reincarnation of one of Buddhism's most famous teachers, Naropa, who lived in the 8th century. This made an indelible impact on me and when I returned home that night I sat at my typewriter and wrote the following:

The Lama and the Small Green Leaf

The small green leaf hung motionless. It was on a bough of a gnarled and twisted tree at the Atisha Buddhist Centre, near Eaglehawk.

184

The air was hot and humid, and on nearby acacia blossoms bees scurried after nectar ahead of the approaching rain.

Near the tree I sat quietly on a paint- blistered seat outside the bedroom of a visiting Buddhist lama. He was giving interviews and although I had not made an appointment his secretary had popped out and with a beatific smile said: "His Holiness will see you in a minute."

His holiness, to give him his full name, was His Holiness the 12th Gyalwang Drugchen, Jigme Pema Wangchen. His gold-emblazoned visiting card, which he gave me later, also carried the nickname "Jimmy." No doubt this was a concession to the occidental inability to handle oriental tongue-twisters.

The waiting minutes seemed to stretch interminably and in my boredom my eyes were drawn to that old tree and in particular to that small green leaf. No matter which way I looked my attention came back to that leaf.

I had heard that if you concentrate hard enough on a object you can "become" the object you are thinking about. Who has not been partially mesmerised by the sound of rain beating on a roof, or been drawn into another thought world by the flickering flames of a fire. Worth a try? There was time to spare. Perhaps I could become that leaf?

As I studied the leaf with increased awareness it seemed to grow in size and in greenness. I concentrated harder. Its border became a line of geometrical beauty, marred only in one spot by a hungry insect.

The network of veins, like those on the hand of a new-born child, were a wonder of delicate tracery.

In the green I began to see other subtle hues - of cobalt blue, alizarin crimson, ochre and in the shadows, slight touches of indigo. So lost was I in my heightened awareness that the heat, the sound of the insects and the ridged hardness of the seat went unnoticed.

Suddenly I started. Was I on the verge of actually becoming that leaf? Had I at last achieved that breakthrough when the mind lifts beyond consciousness and enters the realm of the intuition where symbols have no meaning and understanding comes in wordless concepts?

> *Where:*
> > *Light explodes creating darkness;*
> > *Sound roars in noiseless thunder;*
> > *Perfume wafts from scentless flowers;*
> > *and The plunging eagle hangs motionless.*

The green leaf was part of the tree and it was part of the environment. I was there waiting, and also part of the same environment. It followed therefore that, even if tenuously, I was physically linked with the tree and its small green leaf. In the world of metaphysics the leaf and I were one, just as I was part of the seat on which I was sitting waiting to speak with "Jimmy."

My mind moved to this 25-year-old lama whose age could have made him my son. What was so special about him that he should be called "Holiness." Was he really the reincarnation of the famous seventh-century mystic, Naropa, whose teachings are regarded as second only to those of the Buddha himself. A sceptical thought arose, but then if his authenticity has been affirmed by the Dalai Lama, who crowned him Lord Abbot of a huge monastic order at the age of three who was I to argue?

Time began to drag and my awareness dimmed but once again it was arrested by that small green leaf. It hung there, poised, pristine, exquisitely beautiful and although alone still an integral part of the tree. Who could deny that this leaf was composed of all the subtle essences which comprise the world conceived by our senses?

186

The green leaf twisted slightly in a zephyr breeze then resumed its previous position. One moment it had moved and in moving had become silver, then reverted to green again. Had it changed or for a moment had become an illusion? Which was real, the green leaf or the silver leaf?

Which is the real world, the one understood by our senses or is there another? In all the great religions of the world there is the underlying dictum of an existence beyond. All would agree with the Buddha's teaching at Benares 2,500 years ago that "Buddhas are but fingers pointing the way."

Scientists have proven beyond doubt that our conscious world - everybody and everything in it - is nothing more than vibrating energy slowly evolving under the control of an immutable law of harmony.

As energy must originate somewhere what is the source of this energy of which we are composed? Can it be likened to some vast ocean whose latent power is expressed in the seeming chaos of waves beating on a rocky shore? In this life are we, as described in that famous work, The Voice of Silence, "dewdrops merging with the shining sea?"

Could my awareness at that moment be likened to a fleeting understanding of what Christians means by the "God within" and the Buddhists, by, "Look within, thou are Buddha?"

Is that "shining sea" the true reality, and conscious awareness a mere illusory part - the spindrift along that rocky shore?

In this reality are we all inseparable parts of a whole, so aptly symbolised by the Yin-Yang symbol Does such a concept of integrity, seen against a background of cosmic harmony, explain human bonding - love, compassion, empathy, sacrifice, friendship, and of course their opposites?

The door opened and His Holiness beckoned to me. I removed my shoes and entered. The son sat on a cushion at the feet of the father, though in age the father could have been the son.

Meanwhile, outside the small green leaf hung motionless.

Appendix 1

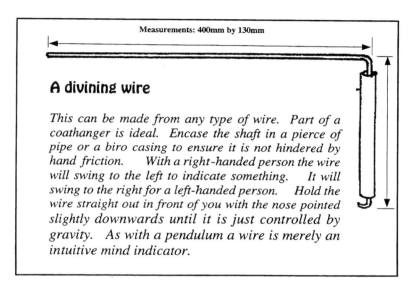

Measurements: 400mm by 130mm

A divining wire

This can be made from any type of wire. Part of a coathanger is ideal. Encase the shaft in a pierce of pipe or a biro casing to ensure it is not hindered by hand friction. With a right-handed person the wire will swing to the left to indicate something. It will swing to the right for a left-handed person. Hold the wire straight out in front of you with the nose pointed slightly downwards until it is just controlled by gravity. As with a pendulum a wire is merely an intuitive mind indicator.

Pendulums

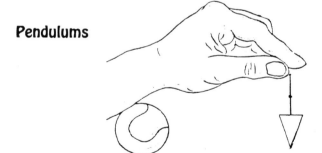

Pendulums can be made out of anything as, like divining wires, they are only an intuitive-mind indicator. When map divining, rest the wrist on a tennis ball for comfort. In all operations set the pendulum moving back and forwards. It will switch to a side movement when it indicates something.

Appendix 2

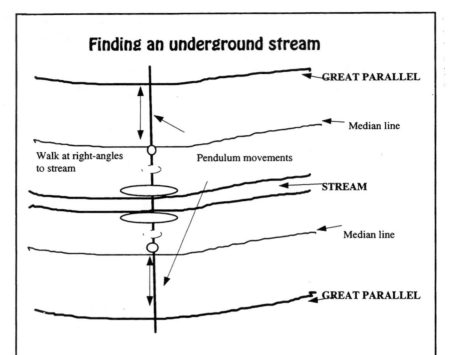

Finding an underground stream

GREAT PARALLEL

Median line

Walk at right-angles to stream

Pendulum movements

STREAM

Median line

GREAT PARALLEL

Finding a stream: *Walk towards the stream with the pendulum oscillating in front of you. It will swing sideways at the **Great Parallel line** then resume oscillating back and forwards until it strikes the **Median Line** when it will begin gyrations which will change to elipses and then to oscillations at the edge of the stream. Repeat the process from the other side. Over the stream the pendulum will move back and forwards. The direction of the oscillations of the pendulum will indicates the stream's flow direction and strength. An L-wire will swing sideways at each line and at the stream edge, and also give the flow direction.*

Appendix 3

Depthing a stream

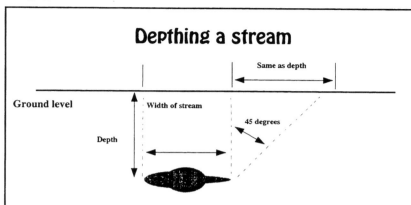

Having found an undergreound stream, simply walk away from it at 90 degrees to the bank and at a certain point your wire or pendulum will swing sideways. The distance from the stream's edge to this point will be the depth. This system is known as "Bishop's Rule." Why it works is still not known but it is believed to have been originated by a French priest who was an expert diviner and named in honor of his Bishop.

Affinity between substances

Many diviners, including Tony Gerovich, of Albany, West Australia, find their ability to locate substances increases when they hold a "sample" in one hand. The most logical explanation for this is that any two substances which are the same emit identical molecular radiations and the diviner is able to "tune" into this affinity. The naturally occuring resonance between substances is of value to diviners in fixing the direction of one subtance from another. You can test this by placing two coins on a table and tracing the lines of resonance between them with a pendulum. When a third coin is introduced the lines bend as influenced by some vectoring effect, the same as gravity bends light rays.

Appendix 4

Map Divining in the Field

STEP 1

Mark the approximate position of the target on your map. Calculate from the scale the distance you need to travel to get near the target. Mark the direction of north on your map and take a compass bearing from your starting point to the approximate target position.

Bearing, say 260 degrees east.

Approximate position of target   **Starting point**

STEP 2

In the field. *When you are about 20 m from your target make a sketch map on a pad. Place three pegs at 1m apart to form an equilateral triangle. Draw triangle to scale on sketch map. Locate target from triangle on map. Measure angle from north and distance to target.*

Target

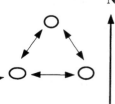

Pegs 1m apart

Appendix 5

Experiments with and opals

Formulas: $R = \dfrac{X2 + Y2}{2Y2}$

$Z = R - Y$

Plan

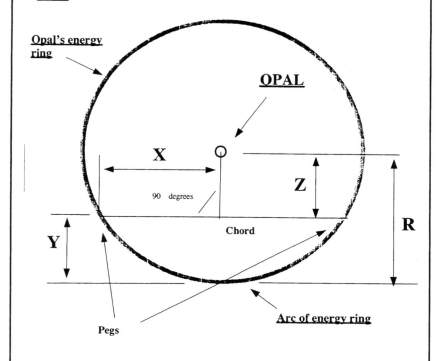

Opal's energy ring

OPAL

X

90 degrees

Z

Chord

R

Y

Arc of energy ring

Pegs

1. Locate energy ring with pendulum or wire
2. Peg and measure half of chord (X)
3. Measure depth of chord (Y)
4. Calculate R
5. Deduct Y from R.

Appendix 5   (continued)

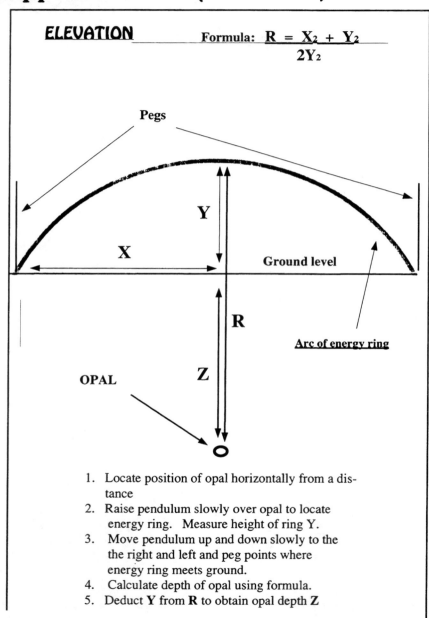

ELEVATION

Formula: $R = \dfrac{X_2 + Y_2}{2Y_2}$

Pegs

Y

X

Ground level

R

Arc of energy ring

OPAL

Z

O

1. Locate position of opal horizontally from a distance
2. Raise pendulum slowly over opal to locate energy ring.   Measure height of ring **Y**.
3. Move pendulum up and down slowly to the the right and left and peg points where energy ring meets ground.
4. Calculate depth of opal using formula.
5. Deduct **Y** from **R** to obtain opal depth **Z**

Appendix 6

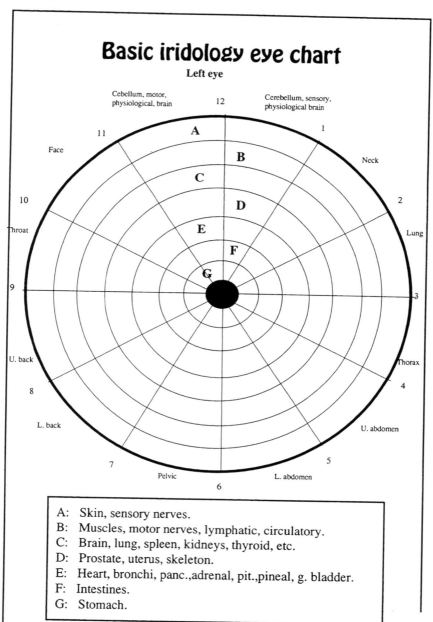

Basic iridology eye chart

Left eye

Cebellum, motor, physiological, brain

12

Cerebellum, sensory, physiological brain

11

1

Face

Neck

A

B

C

10

2

D

Throat

E

Lung

F

G

9

3

U. back

Thorax

8

4

L. back

U. abdomen

7

5

Pelvic

L. abdomen

6

A: Skin, sensory nerves.
B: Muscles, motor nerves, lymphatic, circulatory.
C: Brain, lung, spleen, kidneys, thyroid, etc.
D: Prostate, uterus, skeleton.
E: Heart, bronchi, panc.,adrenal, pit.,pineal, g. bladder.
F: Intestines.
G: Stomach.

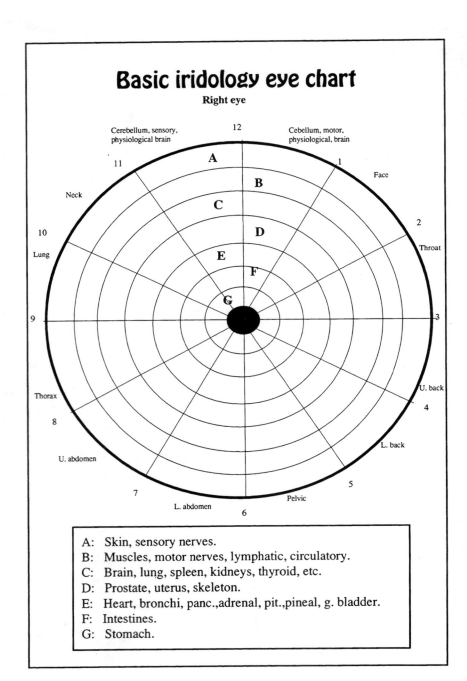

Basic iridology eye chart
Right eye

Cerebellum, sensory, physiological brain

Cebellum, motor, physiological, brain

12

11

1

Face

A

B

Neck

C

10

2

D

Lung

Throat

E

F

9

G

3

U. back

Thorax

4

8

L. back

U. abdomen

5

7

Pelvic

L. abdomen

6

A: Skin, sensory nerves.
B: Muscles, motor nerves, lymphatic, circulatory.
C: Brain, lung, spleen, kidneys, thyroid, etc.
D: Prostate, uterus, skeleton.
E: Heart, bronchi, panc.,adrenal, pit.,pineal, g. bladder.
F: Intestines.
G: Stomach.

Appendix 7

Bibliography

Archdale, F.A. *Elementary Radiesthesia*. British Society of
Dowsers, 1950.

Barret, Sir W & Besterman, T. *The Divining Rod*. University
Books Inc, 1968.

Bentov, I. *Stalking the Wild Pendulum*. Wildood House, 1978.

Bird, C. *The Divining Hand*. New Age Press, Black Mountain,
USA, 1979.

Blackburn, G. *The Science and Art of the Pendulum*. Idylwild
Books, 1983.

Klimentov, Prof.P.P *General Hydrogeology*. MIR Publishers,
1983.

Mermet, Abbet. *Priciples and Practice of Radiesthesia*.
Watkins, 1935.

Rothman, Dr M.A. *The Laws of Physics*. Fawcett World
Library, USA.

Schwartz, S.A. *The Secret Vaults of Time*. Grosset & Dunlap,
USA.

Scott-Elliot, CB, CBE, Maj.-Gen (Rtd), J. *One Man's Way*.

Vriend, J, *Eyes Talk*. Lothian. Melbourne, Australia.

Westlake, Dr A T. *The Pattern of Health*. Shambala, 1973.

The End

Let every man prove his work,
and then shall he have rejoicing in himself alone,
and not in another. For every man shall bear his own burden.
Be not deceived; God is not mocked,
for whatsoever a man soweth that shall he also reap.
For he that soweth to his flesh shall of his flesh
reap corruption; but he that soweth to the spirit
shall reap life ever lasting.

From the letters of St. Paul.

FREE DETAILED CATALOGUE

A detailed illustrated catalogue is available on request, SAE or International Postal Coupon appreciated. Titles are available direct from Capall Bann, post free in the UK (cheque or PO with order) or from good bookshops and specialist outlets. Title currently available include:

Animals, Mind Body Spirit & Folklore
Angels and Goddesses - Celtic Christianity & Paganism by Michael Howard
Arthur - The Legend Unveiled by C Johnson & E Lung
Auguries and Omens - The Magical Lore of Birds by Yvonne Aburrow
Book of the Veil The by Peter Paddon
Call of the Horned Piper by Nigel Jackson
Cats' Company by Ann Walker
Celtic Lore & Druidic Ritual by Rhiannon Ryall
Compleat Vampyre - The Vampyre Shaman: Werewolves & Witchery by Nigel Jackson
Crystal Clear - A Guide to Quartz Crystal by Jennifer Dent
Earth Dance - A Year of Pagan Rituals by Jan Brodie

Earth Magic by Margaret McArthur
Enchanted Forest - The Magical Lore of Trees by Yvonne Aburrow
Healing Homes by Jennifer Dent
Herbcraft - Shamanic & Ritual Use of Herbs by Susan Lavender & Anna Franklin
In Search of Herne the Hunter by Eric Fitch
Inner Space Workbook - Developing Counselling & Magical Skills Through the Tarot
Kecks, Keddles & Kesh by Michael Bayley
Living Tarot by Ann Walker
Magical Incenses and Perfumes by Jan Brodie
Magical Lore of Animals by Yvonne Aburrow
Magical Lore of Cats by Marion Davies

Magical Lore of Herbs by Marion Davies
Masks of Misrule - The Horned God & His Cult in Europe by Nigel Jackson
Mysteries of the Runes by Michael Howard
Oracle of Geomancy by Nigel Pennick
Patchwork of Magic by Julia Day
Pathworking - A Practical Book of Guided Meditations by Pete Jennings
Pickingill Papers - The Origins of Gardnerian Wicca by Michael Howard
Psychic Animals by Dennis Bardens
Psychic Self Defence - Real Solutions by Jan Brodie
Runic Astrology by Nigel Pennick
Sacred Animals by Gordon MacLellan
Sacred Grove - The Mysteries of the Forest by Yvonne Aburrow
Sacred Geometry by Nigel Pennick
Sacred Lore of Horses The by Marion Davies
Sacred Ring - Pagan Origins British Folk Festivals & Customs by Michael Howard
Secret Places of the Goddess by Philip Heselton
Talking to the Earth by Gordon Maclellan
Taming the Wolf - Full Moon Meditations by Steve Hounsome
The Goddess Year by Nigel Pennick & Helen Field
West Country Wicca by Rhiannon Ryall
Witches of Oz The by Matthew & Julia Phillips

Capall Bann is owned and run by people actively involved in many of the areas in which we publish. Our list is expanding rapidly so do contact us for details on the latest releases. We guarantee our mailing list will never be released to other companies or organisations.

Capall Bann Publishing, Freshfields, Chieveley, Berks, RG20 8TF

Radiesthesia